CRACKING THE ACADEMIA NUT:
A Guide to Preparing for Your Academic Career

CRACKING THE

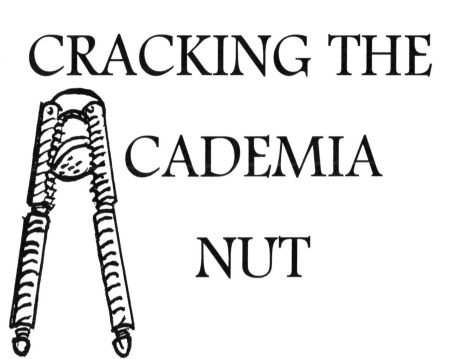

CADEMIA

NUT

A Guide to Preparing for Your Academic Career

Margaret L. Newhouse, Ph.D.
Office of Career Services
Harvard University

Bio

Margaret Locke Newhouse (Ph.D. in Political Science from UCLA) has counseled graduate students and Ph.D.'s at Harvard's Office of Career Services since 1989. She came to this position from a career in education, which includes high school teaching, university and college teaching (UCLA and Scripps College), directing internship programs (Wellesley and Scripps Colleges) that integrated the worlds of academia and work, and coordinating the RAND/UCLA Center for the Study of Soviet International Behavior. She cofounded the Holistic Career Counselors Collaborative and currently maintains a small private practice for career changers. She is the author of *Outside the Ivory Tower: A Guide for Academics Considering Alternative Careers*, published by the Office of Career Services in 1993.

Office of Career Services
Faculty of Arts and Sciences
54 Dunster Street
Harvard University
Cambridge, MA 02138
(617) 495-2595

ISBN 0-943747-18-X

Contents

PART II

THE ACADEMIC JOB SEARCH

PART III

THE JOB OFFER AND BEYOND

Acknowledgments

This book started as a revision and combination of its predecessors, *Preparing for Your Academic Career in the Humanities and Social Sciences* by Cynthia Packert and Martha P. Leape and *Developing Your Career as a Scientist in Academe: A Guide for Prospective Graduate Students, Graduate Students and Ph.D.'s* by Gina Moser, Ph.D., both published by the Office of Career Services (OCS) of the Faculty of Arts and Sciences at Harvard University in 1989. However, it ended up as largely a new book. Not only have market and other conditions changed in the intervening eight years but, in addition, my own interactions with hundreds of graduate students in counseling sessions and workshops, as well as with dozens of faculty members, have inevitably informed this account. Nonetheless, much of the structure and some of the language of the Packert/Leape book have been retained in this one, a testament to the lasting value of their work. My thanks to Cynthia Atherton (formerly Packert), Gina Moser, and Marty Leape, in her roles as both author and former OCS Director.

I am especially grateful to the Harvard students and faculty who have helped re-educate me about the academic job search over these past eight years. Many Harvard professors have served over the years on an annual OCS panel entitled "Securing Your First Academic Position: the Search Committee's View." They are too numerous to acknowledge individually, but several are mentioned in the text, and they all have my gratitude. Special thanks, however, are due to Professors Mark Kishlanksy of the History Department and Stephen Kosslyn of the Psychology Department, not only for generally influencing my approach but also for giving me invaluable feedback on the penultimate draft. I also appreciate Dean Christoph Wolff's taking the time to look at and respond to the final draft. The Graduate School of Arts and Sciences (GSAS) students have been inspiring to work with and their stories have greatly enriched this guide. Regrettably, most—including those who willingly shared their c.v.'s and cover letters—must remain anonymous, but they know, I hope, that they provide the most important satisfaction of my job.

Thanks are also due to the authors of the books and articles I consulted in the process of writing this book, who are separately acknowledged in footnotes. However, special mention should be made of Mary Heiberger and Julie Vick's classic *The Academic Job Search Handbook.*[1] It is no small serendipity that Mary's daughter Sara Heiberger, until recently a staff assistant at OCS, provided outstanding and indispensable editorial and production assistance on this project. Her successor Amanda Phillips provided seamless transition assistance for the final stages, including helping to create the cover. Thanks to Amanda, Jay Vithalani, and Stacey Collins for proofreading the text and making helpful editorial suggestions. Thanks also to Brian Floca for providing cover drawings on short notice. My work-study student Yen-Rong Chen has also provided valuable assistance, particularly in creating the bibliography and appendix on associations. OCS editor Karen From's acute, experienced editorial eye, high standards, and practical sense have substantially improved the final version; however, we both still view this as a work in progress and hope to include more personal stories in a future update. Finally, the support of OCS Director Bill Wright-Swadel for this project, as well as more generally, has been very important to me.

1. Mary Morris Heiberger and Julia Miller Vick, *The Academic Job Search Handbook*, 2d ed. (Philadelphia: University of Pennsylvania Press, 1996).

Introduction

Gone are those nearly mythical days when graduate students could ignore professional development until just before their job search and still expect plum tenure-track positions to fall into their laps. Moreover, the predictions of a dramatic improvement in the academic job market by the mid-90s made in the Bowen Report have not materialized.[1] Although demographic trends still argue for an improvement in the market because they indicate a greater demand for professors, other phenomena are softening their impact. These include reduced federal funding for higher education in general and for scientific research in particular; reduced state commitments to public universities; institutional cost-cutting measures that increase reliance on temporary, part-time, and nontenure-track faculty; and a backlog of qualified job applicants.

As depressed academic job markets lead to increasingly frustrating and demoralizing job searches, graduate students and professors alike are realizing that the career development process needs to begin early in graduate school and requires strategic planning and proactive efforts. This book seeks to get you started on the path

1. See William G. Bowen and Neil R. Rudenstine, *In Pursuit of the Ph.D.* (Princeton: Princeton University Press, 1992), which reiterates the predictions of the original 1989 Bowen and Sosa report. For more recent assessments of trends, consult Jack H. Schuster, "Whither the Faculty? The Changing Academic Labor Market," *Educational Record* 76, no. 4 (fall 1995): 28-33, and "Speculating about the Labor Market for Academic Humanists: 'Once More unto the Breach,'" *Profession 95* (New York: The Modern Language Association of America, 1995), 56-61. For information on the current situation, browse through the *Chronicle of Higher Education*. For Harvard-specific information on Ph.D. employment, see Margaret Newhouse, *Report on Ph.D. Recipients, 1995-96* (Cambridge: Office of Career Services, Faculty of Arts and Sciences, Harvard University, 1996).

1

of professional development and to guide you through the actual job-search process and its aftermath. The assumption is that, despite a lackluster job market and the vagaries of the hiring process, committed new Ph.D.'s who plan carefully and approach the search confidently can substantially increase their chances of getting a good job. It is a grueling process, requiring much time, effort, and psychological resilience, and it may take more than one try before you land the right job. But for those committed to academic careers, it is worth all the effort.

A word of caution: Use this book only as a general guide. Each discipline has its own conventions and procedures; therefore, your best source of information and advice is in your departments—from faculty and your own colleagues who have already tested the waters. In addition, you can get advice and information—not to mention discipline-specific assistance—through your professional associations. On the other hand, because the advice offered in these pages is culled from many and varied sources, this book may offer ideas and perspectives that you would not get from your department, or it may help you resolve conflicting advice. Where there are great differences between disciplines, particularly between the natural sciences and most other fields, they are noted.

Part I covers the critical topic of professional development, starting from the earliest years of graduate school. Chapter One deals with professional development and strategic planning during graduate school; you are encouraged to read this chapter in conjunction with Cynthia Verba's *Scholarly Pursuits*, available through GSAS.[2] Chapter Two deals briefly with how to make the most of postdoctoral fellowships, emphasizing those in the natural sciences.

Part II—the "meat" of the book—takes you through the academic job-search process, giving concrete and detailed advice. Chapter Three is concerned with the general context and your preliminary decisions, an essential but frequently neglected part of the search. These include clarifying your priorities, preparing psychologically, and understanding the process from both the candidate's

2. Cynthia Verba, *Scholarly Pursuits: A Practical Guide to Academe,* rev. ed. (Cambridge: Graduate School of Arts and Sciences, Harvard University, 1997).

and the search committee's perspective. It also provides a timetable for conducting your search.

Application materials and credentials are the subject of Chapter Four, which also contains sample c.v.'s, dissertation abstracts, and cover letters to use as reference points—i.e., guides but *not* templates—for your own unique versions. Chapter Five covers the interview process, both the preliminary interviews conducted by many disciplines at their annual professional meetings, and the "crown jewel"—the campus visit and job talk.

Part III, The Job Offer and Beyond, is devoted to negotiating the job offer and contingency planning if there is no acceptable offer (Chapter Six), and to a brief consideration of how to navigate the first year so that your career gets off to a thriving start (Chapter Seven).

At whatever stage you may be in graduate school or your academic career, the hope is that you will find this guide encouraging and useful as you create your own career path.

Part I

Professional Development as a Graduate Student or Postdoctoral Fellow

Chapter One

Professional Development and Strategic Planning in Graduate School

With some foresight and awareness, you can plan academic and professional activities during graduate school that will greatly enhance your future career. The simple fact is that Ph.D. candidates who have a record of publishing and professional presentations are more likely to receive job offers. It may seem daunting to start planning while you still are faced with the "obstacle course" of academic and language requirements, qualifying papers, general examinations, and thesis research, not to mention teaching. But, although nothing is guaranteed, early strategic planning and conscious professional development throughout graduate school will substantially strengthen your candidacy on the job market.

While strategic planning is necessary, it is hardly sufficient. Self-knowledge is also essential: knowing your own passions, values, and priorities; being open to changing them in the light of new information and opportunities; and being unwilling to compromise them merely for the sake of strategic advantage. It is an ongoing challenge to achieve a balance between integrity ("To thine own self be true") and pragmatism in the service of future employment. And, of course, Lady Luck usually plays a role.

Take time now, and periodically throughout your search, to ask yourself the following questions: What are your most important values? What subjects and issues most excite you? What appeals to you most and least about an academic career? What kind of institution would you like to teach at and what activities do you most enjoy (teaching, mentoring, research, writing, administration)? What are your long- and short-range goals? (See Chapter Three for exercises relating to institutional choice and the work environment.)

This is also a good time to give some thought to alternative careers, both to test your commitment to academia and to increase your options in a tight market. You may want to arrange for nonacademic internships or summer jobs during the early years of graduate school and talk with alumni/ae of the graduate school and others who have taken nontraditional career paths.[1] While it is important to realize that you may be making tradeoffs by not devoting all of your time to academic pursuits, many Ph.D.'s will attest that exploring nonacademic options has a liberating and empowering effect that translates into later success in their academic job searches. As John Fox, a recent Ph.D. in anthropology now teaching at Boston University's College of General Studies, reports, "Interestingly, looking outside my field allowed me to see what I wanted and didn't want for myself, and in the end it landed me a great opportunity within my own field generally, without even moving from Boston!"[2]

Learning About Your Field

One of your primary tasks as you go through your graduate program is to understand the professional dynamics and special characteristics of your discipline. To do this, you should do the following:

- Learn how your field is subdivided and think of how to prepare yourself to straddle boundaries. (The importance of this may vary according to the field.)

1. The Office of Career Services offers a rich variety of programming and career services to Graduate School of Arts and Sciences students considering alternatives to academic careers. See also Margaret Newhouse, Ph.D., *Outside the Ivory Tower: A Guide for Academics Considering Alternative Careers* (Cambridge: Office of Career Services, Faculty of Arts and Sciences, Harvard University, 1993), available at OCS.

2. E-mail to author, May 1997.

- Learn who the major figures are, familiarize yourself with their work, and look for an opportunity to meet them.

- Keep up on relevant literature and journals, and stay abreast of the current issues.

- Learn as early as possible about the timing and requirements of your particular job market.

- Join your professional association(s) right away and attend the meetings when possible. In most cases, the membership rates are considerably lower for students. (Professional associations are listed in Appendix One.)

- Find out about the career paths of your professors, especially those who have been hired recently, and of graduate students who are about to finish. Ask what qualifications they found most important and what strategies they found most useful.

As you begin to clarify your professional direction, think about the strategic implications of your choices. How big a market is there likely to be for your specialty? What can you do to broaden your areas of expertise and hence your appeal? Or, conversely, if you are in an interdisciplinary program, how can you strengthen your credentials in one discipline? It is important to see how you fit into your discipline and related ones, and to develop broad capabilities, particularly if you are aiming for jobs in teaching colleges.

Strive for efficiency as well. You can use seminars to explore areas of specialization and potential dissertation topics. Choose courses and projects that will dovetail with your dissertation as well as fill in gaps in your knowledge.

Choosing Your Research Topic

Consult with your advisers about the advantages and disadvantages of your proposed research topic. Your dissertation will serve two major functions: it will provide you with your rite of passage out of graduate school and it will serve as the source of most of your early publications. Because publishing is important, you need to choose a research topic that you can draw on for a good length of time—especially if you are likely to go straight into teaching without postdoctoral work. In the first year or two of teaching, it is rare to have the time and resources to begin a new area of research. Consequently, it is wise to choose a topic that does not box you in intellectually, but that is broad enough to allow for flexibility and intellectual growth. It also pays to choose a topic that allows you not only to learn from your adviser, but also to establish your own research niche, which becomes identified with you and serves to distinguish you from your adviser.[3]

At the same time, you want to define a manageable topic with clear boundaries, unless you want to spend years trying to produce a definitive magnum opus. Moreover, you will encounter difficulties on the job market if your research is so broad or interdisciplinary that it eludes easy categorization, or if it "falls between the cracks" of certain fields. If, for example, you write a dissertation that straddles anthropology and art history, you will need to decide which department you prefer to work in, and your training should indicate competence in that field. You should also try to avoid becoming too narrowly identified with a particular theoretical or philosophical camp, and especially with a particular proponent. If you do choose a specific line of approach, cultivate other avenues of inquiry that demonstrate intellectual breadth.

A word about procrastination and/or writer's block—familiar topics to many academics. After all, how many graduate students do you know who have completed their dissertations by their original deadlines? One important strategy, related to choosing a manageable topic, is to carefully plan and outline your thesis ahead of time (with the help of your adviser), so that you can work on small segments (chapters or sections of chapters) at a time. But if you find yourself procrastinating on a habitual basis, consider seeking additional help. The Graduate School, some departments, and the Bureau of Study Counsel have "dissertation groups" designed to keep you on track; do not feel embarrassed to participate in them. At the very least, it is important to create a support system—even if

3. I am indebted to Psychology Professor Stephen Kosslyn for putting it in these terms (e-mail to author).

it's only one person—to provide encouragement and counsel and to hold you accountable for meeting self-imposed deadlines.

Networking and Mentors

You'll want to resist any temptation to become passive, withdrawn, or invisible as a graduate student. If you remember that your professors were once graduate students who needed guidance and advice from their own professors, you may find it easier to initiate and maintain contact with them and other leaders in your field. As in any other professional sphere, you need to get to know your future colleagues as early as possible and to participate in professional activities. Start by joining study groups with your peers and participating in graduate student and/or local professional events such as conferences and colloquia. One recent HEAL graduate advises that you tear yourself away from your studies to attend all Harvard seminars and conferences which feature visiting scholars in your field. These experiences will make it easier to work up to the regional and national arenas.

It is even more critical to find a good adviser/mentor or mentors who will provide intellectual and professional guidance throughout your career as a student and ideally beyond, unstinting assistance in the job search, and (ideally) emotional support during the difficult times. Different people benefit from different kinds of relationships and degrees of guidance. The following are some criteria to consider seriously before choosing a dissertation adviser:

- Expertise in your area of interest. (The importance of this may vary by field and circumstance.)

- Prominence and respect within the profession. (This is important—most significantly in the natural sciences—because you will be known as "So-and-So's student.")

- Enthusiasm for you and your work, and a willingness to engage with you intellectually on a regular basis. (This is of key importance and can overcome a lack of expertise if circumstances demand.)

- Likelihood of their staying at Harvard. (However, don't over-value this, since you can stay in regular e-mail contact, assuming they use it, or even move with an adviser, if necessary.)

- Job market savvy and a reputation for actively helping their students develop professionally and get jobs.

- A reputation for helping students finish quickly (or at least within a reasonable time frame).

- A reputation for seeing the big picture and setting goals. (This is particularly important for lab research.)[4]

- An appropriate balance between providing guidance and structure and encouraging you to develop your skills, ideas, and voice independently. Beware of professors at either extreme of the continuum.

- Reputation for integrity and decency (a "mensch").

By all means, do some thorough research on a potential adviser's track record with students and the match between your needs and his or her style. More than a few GSAS students have chosen dissertation advisers despite their poor reputations for mentoring, believing that their relationship would be different or that they could stand it—and then lived to regret their choice.

We live in an imperfect world, however, and you may find you develop a less than ideal relationship with your adviser for a variety of reasons. In that case, take steps to improve the situation. Try every way you know to address the problems directly with your adviser: maintain regular contact, ask for and respond to feedback, discuss the problems as you see them, and brainstorm possible solutions. If things do not improve, you might bring in a third party (the department chair, the Director of Graduate Studies, the Dean of the Graduate School of Arts and Sciences, or the Ph.D. counselors at the Office of Career Services) or, if necessary, change advisers.

Even if you have an ideal adviser, you should cultivate other

4. Peter Feibelman, *A Ph.D. is Not Enough!* (Reading: Addison-Wesley Publishing Company, 1993), 19-20.

supporters, advisers, and mentors among Harvard and other faculties as well as among other graduate students. Junior faculty can be an invaluable resource and are often more accessible than senior faculty.

In the last analysis, however, the responsibility for your career development is yours. With that in mind, be increasingly proactive about your professional development as you make your way through graduate school.

Developing Professional Opportunities During Graduate School

In general, when an institution decides to hire a new faculty member, it will look for a candidate with a stellar academic background who can "hit the ground running," namely, someone who

- is supported by superlative letters of recommendation;
- has done interesting, if not ground-breaking, research that can be extended easily into the future;
- has published in respectable academic journals (this varies by discipline; it is mandatory in the sciences);
- has good teaching experience (definition of "good" varies by institution);
- has won awards and distinctions, including (in some disciplines) research grants; and
- has given lectures and scholarly presentations.

As part of assessing candidates, the search committee members will speculate about their future promise. Do they have the potential to make a contribution to the field, thereby adding to the prestige of the school? Depending on the type of school, the emphasis may be weighted more towards research than teaching, or vice versa, but it will be to your advantage to establish a record that features a good balance of both.

How do you begin to develop an attractive range of professional activities while in graduate school? It may be tempting to become totally immersed in your dissertation research and let the years slide by, but that is unwise. Try to schedule regular appointments with your adviser to review your progress and seek his or her advice. When recommending you for a faculty position, your adviser will evaluate you not only on the quality of your final work, but also on your relationships with members of your department and on your awareness of professional developments beyond your dissertation topic. Thus, you need to demonstrate that you can be productive in your research and be a participant in the department and the profession at the same time.

Fellowships and Grants: Most graduate students, particularly in the humanities and social sciences, will need to supplement their financial aid packages with other fellowships to support their dissertation research and writing, or perhaps to support additional language or other study. Science graduate students may be called upon to write grant proposals to help fund their dissertation research. Although preparing fellowship applications and grant proposals is time-consuming and often frustrating, the results are worth the effort. This is obvious if you receive the funding: you get prestige and c.v. credentials, as well as the money and peace of mind. But even if you are turned down, you develop the proposal writing skills necessary for subsequent attempts and later survival in academia.

Cynthia Verba's *Scholarly Pursuits* gives good advice on graduate and postdoctoral fellowships, as well as professional development, and the GSAS Fellowships Office publishes annual fellowship guides. All are available from GSAS in Byerly Hall.

Publishing: In the beginning, learn to set small, attainable goals for yourself. Develop the habit of valuing each of your products and of realizing them to their full potential. A good place to start is with a seminar paper that has received favorable comments from a professor. In formulating seminar paper topics, try to select something that not only allows you to develop the methodology of your field and do original research but that is also feasible and relatively conclusive. Save the "big topics" for later; for now, develop expertise in producing solid, original, and manageable papers that translate well into journal articles, or that could form part of a catalog or an edited work. Subscribe to journals in your field and subfield, and read them cover to cover so that you can "absorb the conventions of the discipline"[5]—those of substance as well as style and format. If you are not ready to publish in the major journals, you should aim for a smaller, not too obscure publication, but one that is refereed. Book reviews are also a good way to get your name known (and to receive a free book), but they are less valued as publications than articles in known, refereed journals.

As you structure your dissertation research, think in terms of relatively short, complete projects (for scientists and economists particularly) or discrete chapters that will lend themselves to journal publications or conference presentations. Graduate students in the sciences are generally expected to publish their results as each project is completed (usually co-authored with their adviser and/or other colleagues) and then to string a series of such articles together to form the dissertation. Economics students usually write three papers of journal quality in lieu of a traditional dissertation. Expectations for publications thus vary by discipline, but in today's market no one can afford to neglect this area.

Ask for feedback and critical comments from your faculty. It may also be desirable to send your work to outside colleagues for commentary. Above all, learn to ask for advice. Criticism can help you clarify your ideas, assumptions, and conclusions. It also provides opportunities to engage in intellectual debate with your colleagues and professors, which is one of the great pleasures of academic life. On the other hand, don't be discouraged by the tendency in academia to rely on negative criticism more than on positive.

Making Presentations: If a seminar paper is not ready to be submitted to a journal, consider it as a possible topic for a conference or colloquium presentation or for a poster session. Making presentations is good practice, and gives you the chance to get immediate feedback from your colleagues. You can then incorporate their comments if you plan to develop your paper further. You may want to start with a paper at a departmental or interdepartmental colloquium and work your way up to local and regional conferences,

5. Thanks to History Professor Mark Kishlansky for this turn of phrase (communication with author).

which are frequently more relaxed and accessible than the large national conferences. Even if you have not been asked to participate on a panel, the organizers may accept individual papers. If you find that your work does not fit the themes of the conference panels, consider organizing your own session, with the help of more experienced colleagues or professors.

Eventually, you will probably want to submit a proposal to your professional association's annual conference; for deadlines, check the association's journal, the *Chronicle for Higher Education*, and/or with your department. Many departments, as well as the Harvard Graduate Society, have some funding to cover conference expenses for graduate students, especially if you are presenting. Departments may also offer venues for practice runs of your presentations.

Whatever the forum for the conference, be sure you find out what to expect. For example: Will you sit or stand? Speak from notes or read a paper? Answer questions at a poster session? How long should you speak? Is there a discussant for your paper? A moderator? Will there be questions from the audience? What should you wear? Should you prepare handouts? Should you or can you use overheads or slides? Are there size restrictions on posters? (Check the section on job talks in Chapter Five for some practical advice that also applies to conference presentations.) After you have presented a paper or a poster session, be sure to write down the names of people who seem interested in your work and follow up with them after the conference.

Even when you are not presenting a paper yourself, you should make a practice of attending presentations and conferences in your field, especially at Harvard or other local institutions. Although they may seem like yet another interruption to your research, they are valuable for several reasons: you may learn something, you can make professional contacts, you will gain insights that make it easier for you to prepare presentations of your own, and, by participating in the discussion after the presentation, you will have another opportunity to become known in your chosen field.

Expanding Your Network: It is a fact of professional life—in academia and elsewhere—that establishing and maintaining a professional network will greatly enhance your career development.

Attendance at conferences, particularly the annual national meetings, offers you further opportunities to learn about the field at large and to broaden your acquaintances. If possible, ask your adviser or other professors to introduce you to those colleagues with whom you share professional interests. If you are on your own, it may seem artificial and awkward at first to approach scholars whom you don't know, but it is important to become comfortable with introducing yourself and establishing professional relationships where there are legitimate shared interests and you are not simply "sucking up." This may seem more natural in established contexts of shared interests: for example, sessions that relate to your research, interest group meetings (such as women's groups), or informal departmental receptions (your own, or perhaps your undergraduate institution's). Consider arranging in advance to meet with someone whose work particularly interests you.

Remember, you are not "merely a graduate student"—you are a Ph.D. candidate and a junior colleague. It is in your best interest to be cordial, confident, and professional at all times; you will be meeting these people time after time in various professional capacities. Even if you are on the academic market, you should not appear too anxious to discuss job opportunities; there are other avenues for discovering job openings. If you do learn in conversation of an interesting opening, make discreet inquiries about the proper channels for application.

Conferences are also a good place to learn the agenda for future meetings. If you find out what the topics for the following year's sessions will be, then you have more lead time to prepare something for submission. Two practical hints: make your reservations early so you can stay in the main conference hotel, where most of the action is, and wear your nametag at all times.

Networking today, particularly in the natural sciences, is largely done through the Internet. If you haven't done so already, introduce yourself to the vast resources and communication potential of this new technology. If you don't want to explore on your own, go to the Widener reference librarian for a demo or ask a friend to get you started. It is still possible and sometimes preferable to call or write to potential colleagues whose work you admire, but you increasingly put yourself at a disadvantage if you are "electronically challenged."

Teaching: If you are in the humanities and many of the social sciences, teaching and lecturing will occupy much of your time in graduate school, once you have completed your course requirements. In the sciences, it is possible, but generally not desirable, to avoid teaching altogether. The team effort of being one of the teaching fellows for a large lecture course provides a good opportunity to receive guidance and learn from others' experiences. If your department offers you a choice, consider requesting to lead a tutorial or seminar on your own; these are good forums for developing your own syllabi and reading lists and for directing individual papers. You could broaden your experience by advising a senior thesis and/ or by giving guest lectures in a course. Serving as Head Teaching Fellow also provides invaluable education in how to administer a course.

The Bok Center for Teaching and Learning is a superb resource for developing and strengthening your teaching skills. By all means take advantage of its numerous programs and services, including two-day orientation programs each semester and the opportunity to have them videotape and critique individual classes. They can also help with constructing teaching portfolios, which are a relatively new tool for gathering and presenting your teaching "credentials" so as to enhance your candidacy on the job market. Students who have participated in the Bok Center's Writing Fellows program have found it to be a selling point in an era of declining writing skills.

Teaching experience outside Harvard also strengthens your c.v. If you have the chance to teach a course elsewhere, consider it seriously, especially if it pays well and does not take too much time away from your dissertation research. Similarly, being a guest lecturer in a colleague's class is not only fun, but also a good way to become acquainted with another campus and classroom environment. (You can expect compensation for your expenses, and occasionally you may receive an honorarium for your efforts.) You stand to gain several things: some welcome perspective, the opportunity to learn to do things in a non-Harvard way, and perhaps some outside professional recommendations. While Harvard's prestige may make you a desirable candidate, many institutions will be impressed with a demonstrated ability to function well outside the Harvard environment.

Getting Administrative Experience: As a professor, most of your professional work will focus on teaching and research, but it will also include a variety of administrative activities. These may range from attending standard departmental meetings to serving on committees on hiring, administrative planning, admissions, curriculum, and a host of other issues. Obtaining some administrative experience as a graduate student gives you an opportunity to familiarize yourself with the process, develop your organizational and managerial skills, and perhaps gain a competitive edge as a job candidate. Examples include becoming an officer or an active member of the Graduate Council or your departmental graduate society. Some departments include graduate student representatives on faculty selection committees; this offers a unique opportunity to learn how your department formulates its hiring needs and criteria. Becoming a head Teaching Fellow for a course is an excellent administrative training ground, and serving as a House tutor, especially a House Fellowships Adviser, offers rich experience in formal student advising, as well as administration.

Making Your Department and Harvard University Work for You: Several departments have institutionalized programs to help "professionalize" their students. Take advantage of every resource available to you, and if your department doesn't offer a program that you would find valuable, try lobbying for it or even organizing it. Also explore other resources for professional development at Harvard, especially the Office of Career Services, the Graduate School of Arts and Sciences, and the Bok Center. The following is a list of the resources which some departments offer:

- *Department newsletters* with information about upcoming lectures and events, social functions, news of individuals, and announcements of deadlines for fellowship competitions and meetings. Some also list job openings.

- *Job binders or books with current job and fellowship listings.*

- *Graduate study colloquia,* which address how to meet degree requirements and how to prepare for general examinations.

- *Dissertation colloquia,* which give students perspective on the process and keep them on track. Meetings may be devoted to discussing content, working out problems, generating outlines, developing short and long versions of abstracts, and presenting work, from rough chapters to job talks.

- *Professional colloquia,* which address course and syllabus development and the "how-tos" of teaching and grading, lectures and presentations, and sometimes writing and publishing. The model program is the Psychology Department's biennial credit seminar entitled "The Real World," which includes sessions on all aspects of professional development in graduate school and beyond, as well as ones on the job search (see Appendix Two).

- *Job-search or placement meetings,* which address the academic job-search process and offer advice and guidance to graduate students going on the market. Some departments also hold mock interviews. Faculty advisers generally assist their students with the development of c.v.'s and letters of application, and—if asked—preparation for interviews and seminar or job-talk presentations.

- *Resume books,* distributed to colleges and universities and other potential employers, which are now on-line in a couple of enterprising departments.

As you begin to incorporate professional experiences into your graduate program, create a curriculum vitae (c.v. or vita) to record them. Also, gather reference letters from faculty with whom you have established rapport and with whom you expect to work further; they can update their letters periodically. Finally, be sure to keep your advisers and other colleagues informed of your progress—not only your dissertation timetable, but also your other professional activities. In summary, become a participating citizen in your department and in your professional field as early as you possibly can.

Chapter Two

Postdoctoral Fellowships

Postdoctoral fellowships have long constituted the standard route from graduate school to faculty positions for the natural sciences and "hard" behavioral sciences like experimental psychology. Today, because of the difficult academic market, scientists often find themselves taking two or three postdocs before landing a faculty position.[1] They are the essential launching pad for an academic career (even in a teaching college); therefore, this chapter focuses on science postdocs.

First, though, a word to social scientists and even humanists, who are increasingly finding postdocs to be a way station to the tenure-track job. Although they can be viewed as "hedging your bets," postdoctoral fellowships can jump-start an academic career by providing time to present at professional meetings, bring out publications, get new research into the pipeline, and generally expand academic networks. Postdocs for humanists and social scientists are usually offered by a specific organization, like the National Endowment for the Humanities, or an institution such as Harvard's Junior Fellowships.[2] These require a fellowship proposal that both fits the funder's "vision" and describes your own original project.

1. William F. Massy and Charles A. Goldman, *The Production and Utilization of Science and Engineering Doctorates in the U.S.* (Palo Alto: Stanford Institute for Higher Education Research, 1995).

2. For fellowship listings, see: the GSAS Fellowship Office, its *Guide to Postdoctoral Fellowships*, OCS (where relatively few are listed), your department office, your advisers, your professional association and journals, the Internet (start with http://www.fas.harvard.edu/~fasocs/Funding/links.htm, and http://www.cs.yale.edu/HTML/YALE/CS/HyPlans/tap/fellowships.html).

Note that this kind of proposal may require a great deal of effort on your part. It usually will *not* suffice to revise your dissertation for publication. The deadlines generally coincide with intense pressure to finish your dissertation, apply for jobs, teach, or fulfill other obligations and commitments; but, if you wish to apply, grit your teeth and tell yourself that each task reinforces the others. Seek advice and help from your advisers; the GSAS Fellowships Adviser; *The Harvard Guide to Postdoctoral Fellowships*,[3] *Scholarly Pursuits* (both available at Byerly Hall), and other directories available at OCS or on-line; your professional association; and peers who have successfully navigated the process. This advice applies as well to those *natural* scientists who are applying for institutional postdoctoral fellowships (e.g., the National Science Foundation and the Lawrence Livermore National Laboratory).

According to Peter Feibelman's excellent book *A Ph.D. is Not Enough!*,[4] a postdoctoral fellowship in academia, industry, or government labs provides would-be research scientists with the opportunity to accomplish three essential tasks:

- to decide in what area you will make your name,

- to finish at least one significant project, and

- to establish your identity in the research community sufficiently to get a job as an assistant professor or in a lab.

There are two classes of postdocs: (1) those that provide further development of your thesis work and corresponding techniques, and (2) those that support a change in direction and/or the development of complementary skills and expertise. You must decide which best serves your needs. In the first case, it is crucial to get up and running quickly. With suggestions from your adviser and/or other

3. Cynthia Verba, *The Harvard Guide to Postdoctoral Fellowships*, annual publication of the Harvard University Graduate School of Arts and Sciences, Cambridge, Mass.

4. Feibelman, *A Ph.D. is Not Enough!*, 22. I have relied heavily on Feibelman and also on Moser, *Developing Your Career as a Scientist in Academe*, for this chapter, as well as on suggestions from Professors Steven Kosslyn of the Psychology Department, Daniel Fisher of the Physics Department, and Donald Pfister of the Biology Department at Harvard.

mentors and colleagues,[5] look for a position where, as soon as you arrive, you can get to work on a defined and significant research project, preferably including one or more short-term projects, and *not* one for which completely new techniques are still being developed. If you choose the second path, you will have to devote more time to additional training and getting a project going, but the payoff can be to carve out a more personally and professionally rewarding niche in research.

Another way to classify postdocs is by source of funding. If you get the funding yourself (via a fellowship), you usually have more freedom to develop your own research agenda than if you are supported by an adviser's grant; however, this depends entirely on the supervisor, so in some labs it may not be true.[6]

Philosophies also differ on what constitutes the "ideal" adviser. Some people, including Feibelman, suggest looking for a mature scientist who won't feel the need to compete with you and who will be supportive of your career. Others see advantages to younger advisers, who might spend more time in the lab and better appreciate your needs as a postdoctoral fellow. In either case, you should try to find someone who takes mentoring seriously.

Usually your thesis or other advisers can make inquiries for postdoctoral positions on your behalf. Sometimes all you will need to do to land a research position is to send a vita, research abstract, and brief letter, followed by a phone conversation. Other times you will have to make a stronger case for yourself, by presenting your thesis research well in an on-site seminar and otherwise demonstrating that you are a productive and collaborative colleague. It is wise to do some research into the labs, including a visit to meet the potential supervisor *and* the current postdocs, in order to get a sense of whether you will have a fruitful, collegial relationship. In fact, it is very risky not to do this.

As a postdoctoral fellow your job is to produce quality results, presentations, and publications and to make yourself known and valued by colleagues outside as well as inside your lab, specialized

---

5. See also the directories and sources listed above and in the Bibliography.

6. Thanks to Psychology Professor Stephen Kosslyn for informing this discussion (e-mails to author).

field, and institution. If possible, you also will establish some independence; you can gain invaluable experience by obtaining funding for and carrying out your own research project. When you are—all too soon—preparing to go on the job market, you will have an impressive vita and enthusiastic references.

Part II

The Academic Job Search

Chapter Three

Preliminaries of Fundamental Importance

As you catch the glimmer of light at the end of the dissertation tunnel, you'll want to begin preparations for the academic job search. This process is multifaceted and involves clarifying your priorities, preparing yourself psychologically, deciding on timing, getting your credentials in order, and, finally, embarking on the actual job search. This chapter covers all the preliminaries, including researching and applying for jobs, but defers a discussion of credentials until the next chapter.

Clarifying Your Priorities and
Evaluating Yourself as a Candidate

Take this opportunity to reconsider the type of institution, work environment, colleagues, and career path you want. Ideally, you would choose your first job with an eye toward your future career and in accordance with your values. Given current market conditions, however, you might also need to consider and even accept positions that are less than ideal and trust that you can make them work for you. The goal is to embrace both flexibility and open-mindedness without sacrificing essential values and goals. For example, one Ph.D. in English and American literature who had had repeated frustrating experiences on the job market decided to let go of all her preconceptions, considered all job possibilities, and was on the verge of accepting a job in a state college in the rural South. Realizing that this would likely preclude any work beyond teaching—work that she cared about and that would allow her to advance professionally—she ultimately decided instead to arrange a nonpaying affiliation with a research center at Harvard. She was then free to apply for a last-minute replacement position at a top-quality liberal arts college in New England, which she parlayed into a tenure-track position after her first year there.

Unfortunately, you may need to compromise on long-term goals for longer than you would wish. A Ph.D. in Russian history, for example, took one postdoctoral year and two yearlong replacement positions, including what he called an unappealing job truly in the boondocks. After these, however, he was able to land a plum job in a large research university.

If you are in a dual-career relationship, these issues become all the more complex. For example, you will need to consider additional options such as under what conditions, if any, you would be willing to have a commuter marriage. Honest self-assessment and attention to priorities, flexibility and the willingness to compromise, and open and candid communication will all ease the process substantially. (Consult Appendix Three for some tips on approaching the job search in dual-career families.)

The following three exercises can help you clarify your priorities:

1. Rank characteristics or factors on a scale from 0-3 from "neutral" to "essential," in terms of their importance to you. If you are in a committed relationship, do them independently and then compare notes with your partner or spouse.

   Where applicable, precede the number with a "+" if a positive influence or advantage, and a "-" if a negative influence or deterrent.

Location[1]

___ part of the country (specify)_____

___ other countries (specify)_____

___ urban

___ small city/suburban

___ small town/rural

___ distance from a major metropolitan or intellectual center
(specify relevant center and/or distance)_____

Institutional Type

___ private

___ public

___ community college

___ small liberal arts college

___ medium-sized university

___ large research university

___ professional school (specify)_____

___ joint appointment (specify)_____

Priorities/Incentives

___ research

___ graduate education/teaching

___ undergraduate education/teaching

Type of Student Body

___ geographic, age, ethnic and/or other representation/diversity
(specify) _____

___ caliber of students

___ residential

___ commuting

___ socioeconomic diversity/percentage on financial aid

___ typical postgraduate career goals

1. The advice here is geared toward U.S. jobs, but foreign nationals may be considering the issue of whether to look in the U.S., their home country, or other countries. U.S. citizens not infrequently find postdoctoral positions abroad and, occasionally, attractive professorial positions.

Special Characteristics/Orientation of Department

___ women's college

___ religious institution (specify) _____

___ intellectual/ideological orientation (specify) _____

___ innovative/experimental curriculum

___ prestige/reputation of department and/or institution

___ high probability of tenure

___ degree of pressure (intense versus merely high)

___ salary level (specify) _____

___ generous leave, sabbatical policy

___ benefits

___ funding for lab, computer, travel, research, library

___ availability of a mentor

___ collegiality of department

2. Evaluate your own strengths and weaknesses as a candidate and as a potential colleague. Do this alone first and then ask your advisers and peers for their input, asking them in particular to describe your special strengths and gifts. (The academic culture is more apt to focus on weaknesses and liabilities.) This will help you to make your case throughout the entire process of writing c.v.'s and cover letters, giving a list of "selling points" to your advisers, and interviewing.

3. You and your adviser may want to discuss your competitiveness for current—or even hypothetical—job openings and follow the rule of applying mainly for "realistic" institutions, with a few "reaches" and "safeties" (if these exist!) thrown in. However, bear in mind the many vagaries of the process, and do not necessarily be deterred from trying for dream jobs. Be forewarned that some advisers and departments rank their candidates and advise applying only to "realistic" options; in this case they may not give good recommendations for what they perceive as reaches. Ultimately you alone must be the judge of your particular situation, but don't be overly timid about applying, especially for jobs that fit well.

Psychological Preparation

Undoubtedly you know from fellow students who have already been on the market how physically and psychologically demanding the job search is. It takes more time, energy, and discipline than you might have imagined to prepare your c.v. and generic cover letter, identify appropriate job openings, and tailor your letter to each job— not to mention preparing for interviews at professional meetings and on-campus visits, putting together a job talk, and going on campus interviews. One recent economics applicant cautions that you can expect to get no substantive work done for six months.

The psychological toll of putting yourself "out there" time after time is more subtle, yet subversive. No matter how much you rationalize rejections, they are painful and demoralizing—even when you end up with a job, as several Harvard faculty members have testified.

Approaching the job search with two basic precepts can help get you through the rough spots:[2]

1. Know that you are in charge of your job search. Although you have every right to receive help and support from your adviser or advisers, you must take the initiative on all fronts, and ultimately you must decide what is right for you.

2. At the same time, recognize that much of this process is out of your control. Many arbitrary and idiosyncratic factors determine an acceptance or rejection, so do not take the inevitable rejections personally, and maintain your sense of humor and perspective.

One last piece of general advice: put together a support network—family, friends, mentors, other faculty who know you, counselors, whomever—and use them shamelessly.

2. Although this is widely disseminated advice, the statement here reflects the presentation by History Professor Mark Kishlansky on a job-search panel organized by the author in October 1994.

Timing

Because the academic job search is highly structured and begins in the fall, your choices regarding timing are limited. The major issue is whether to venture out with a dissertation that won't be
completed by the time of the hiring decision or, at the latest, by
June. In today's market you will most likely be competing against
seasoned candidates who have their degrees in hand, and may have
already held a postdoctoral fellowship (as scientists are almost guaranteed to have done) or a temporary teaching position. Some may
even have a tenure-track position from which they are "trading up."
It's safe to say that, in the absence of special circumstances, you are
unlikely to get a tenure-track job without convincing assurance
that your degree will be in hand by the time you begin. However, these special circumstances can include the "perfect fit,"
so if you come across a particularly appealing job or close match,
go for it.

Opinions differ about the wisdom of applying widely with an
incomplete dissertation: some find the experience helpful for the
next round; others think you damage your reputation by applying
prematurely. There is the additional problem of when, between applying for and beginning a position, you will find the time to finish.
In any case, this is a decision you will make in consultation with
your adviser or advisers, whose full support you will need in this
difficult process.

The Search Process: An Institutional Perspective

The cycle of academic hiring usually begins in October and
concludes by April or May, but the active months vary enormously
by discipline, and to a lesser extent, by institution. Moreover, there
often tends to be a two-tiered system, with tenure-track decisions
made by March and replacement positions filled in April and May,
or even later. Positions are usually announced in the fall, and, depending on the field, screening interviews are held at the annual
professional meetings, which start as early as November and go into

March. The top two to five candidates selected either in the preliminary interviews or directly from the pile of applicants (for those institutions that don't conduct annual meeting interviews) are brought to the campus for intensive interviews, a job talk, and, possibly, a teaching demonstration. Campus visits typically are scheduled as early as January and as late as April, depending on the institution and discipline.

Viewing the process from the perspective of the search committee not only will help you to be more strategic but will also illustrate the arbitrary aspects of the process. Remember that the composition of the search committee may be random, that most if not all of its members will not specialize in your field, and that they may have their own agendas. At the same time, you can assume that they have a stake in selecting a good colleague—one with promise and "fit." Imagine time-pressured professors facing hundreds of applications for one position. In the initial screening round, they are looking for reasons to reject applicants; your job, therefore, is to present an impeccable and compelling application (see Chapter Four for specifics).

The Search Process: From Decision to Application

In today's market, you need to take the long view of the search process, which could extend two or three years. The first time out, you should schedule from fifteen to eighteen months for the entire job-search process, from your initial preparation to the first day on the job. The most important first step is to prepare your academic credentials, which include

- a curriculum vitae (c.v.), including dissertation abstract

- a cover or application letter

- letters of recommendation

- statements of teaching and research interests, and

- additional examples of your work.

A general timetable for jobs beginning in September is presented below. These guidelines are only approximate, as schedules vary according to disciplines, institutions, and other factors. Also keep in mind that this chapter covers only the application stages.

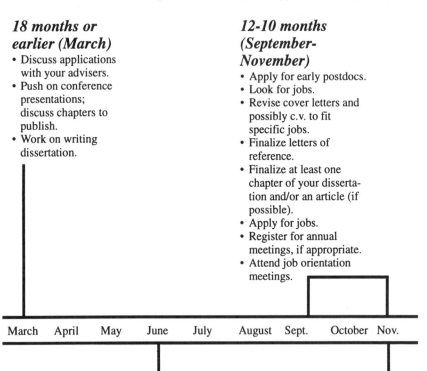

18 months or earlier (March)
- Discuss applications with your advisers.
- Push on conference presentations; discuss chapters to publish.
- Work on writing dissertation.

12-10 months (September–November)
- Apply for early postdocs.
- Look for jobs.
- Revise cover letters and possibly c.v. to fit specific jobs.
- Finalize letters of reference.
- Finalize at least one chapter of your dissertation and/or an article (if possible).
- Apply for jobs.
- Register for annual meetings, if appropriate.
- Attend job orientation meetings.

March   April   May   June   July   August   Sept.   October   Nov.

15 months (June)
- Prepare a draft of your c.v. and dissertation abstract; get feedback.
- Write generic cover letter(s).
- Establish dossier; get references lined up.
- Scout out postdocs.
- WRITE!

10-8 months (November–January)
- Prepare and practice for annual meeting interviews.
- Attend meetings, interview, present, network.
- Prime advisers to network on your behalf and/or make calls for specific jobs.
- Keep looking for postdocs and/or jobs.
- Keep writing (if possible).

8-6 months (January-March)

- Attend late professional meetings.
- Prepare for campus visits.
- Prepare and *practice* job talks.
- Go on campus visits.
- Negotiate early job offers.
- Keep looking for late job/postdoc opportunities.
- Generate fallback options (including postponing degree and applying for Harvard and nonacademic positions).

3 months (June)

- If you have a job and a degree: vacation, move, prepare for teaching.
- If you have a job and aren't quite finished, FINISH the dissertation and prepare for classes.
- If you are still unemployed, lock in your fallback option.

| Dec. | January | Feb. | March | April | May | June | July | August | September |

6-4 months (March-May)

- Go on late campus visits.
- Negotiate job offers.
- Keep looking for options, especially in the secondary job market (part-time and replacement positions).
- Finish dissertation.
- File for degree (if advisable).

September

- Begin your job or postdoc and/or
- Renew your search—it's much easier the second time around!

At least eighteen months in advance, in the spring semester at the latest, consult with your adviser and other faculty members about your preparation for the job market. It is important to make sure you know what your faculty expects from you and what you can expect from them. Seek their advice on how you might strengthen your candidacy. Ask them whether they might mention you favorably to colleagues they know at other institutions who are preparing for a search in your field. You might even ask them to follow the example of Professor Irven DeVore of the Anthropology Department, who regularly sows the seeds for his candidates before searches are formally opened so that job descriptions can be crafted with them in mind.

If you have not given any presentations at professional meetings, find out the deadlines for national, regional, or local meetings and prepare material for submission.

About fifteen months in advance, during the summer, begin work on your written materials. If you have not done so already, prepare a draft of your c.v. and a preliminary dissertation abstract. Consult with your adviser and one of the Ph.D. counselors at the Office of Career Services for feedback on content, format, wording, and clarity.

You may establish a dossier in the OCS Dossier Service and have your letters of recommendation placed on file and sent out from there. Some departments, however, recommend that your letters be sent directly from the department. In this situation, you might want to use the Dossier Service as a back-up. Further information on the Dossier Service can be found in Chapter Four.

Focus on finishing your dissertation or (especially for scientists) on your research program more generally. Remember that in the next academic year you will have much less time to work on it. To restate the obvious: the more complete your dissertation is, the stronger you will be as a candidate. You might aim for a March degree so you can have your Ph.D. in hand when you reach the interview stage. (Be sure you check out the financial implications of the early degree, so that you don't have to sacrifice health insurance, teaching opportunities, etc.)

Twelve months in advance, in the early fall, confirm with your adviser and with all relevant professors and colleagues your intentions of going on the job market. Seek their guidance and support.

Attend any job-search or placement meetings or panels held by your department, the Office of Career Services, or the Graduate School. If there are no meetings scheduled in your department, ask your Director of Graduate Study if you can help to plan one.

Request letters of recommendation from your thesis adviser and from two to four other faculty members at Harvard or other institutions who know your work, with whom you have collaborated on research, and/or who have supervised your teaching. In answer to the frequent question of how many letters to solicit, Government Professor Sidney Verba uses the game-theory concept of "minimum winning coalition." This means that it is better to have three or four very strong letters than a lot of letters in which a less than rave review will carry undue negative weight. The most successful letters of reference reflect the unique qualities that make you stand out from the rest of the candidates. Chapter Four discusses in greater depth ways in which you can help your recommenders write stronger letters.

Prepare final versions of your c.v., dissertation abstract, and generic drafts of cover letters. You may want to reorder or rewrite these materials (and particularly to tailor the cover letter) to change their focus or emphasis when you apply for specific jobs, but it is very helpful to have drafts ready. If possible, finalize at least one chapter of your dissertation and/or an article for later submission as supplementary material.

Researching Job Opportunities

Jobs are listed in a variety of ways throughout the fall and early winter (with part-time replacement positions listed into the spring and summer). In partial response to Equal Employment Opportunity guidelines and because of a desire to move away from the "old boy network," most jobs are listed publicly and nationally. The exception is local positions that do not merit a full-blown national search.

The most consistent and representative source of job listings is your professional association (see Appendix One). If you are not a member, your department should have copies of the latest announcements. Most professional associations now also list their job announcements on their Web sites.

Your department will probably also post notices of job openings that it receives directly. Your professors frequently receive requests for suggestions of appropriate candidates for upcoming positions, which, in the interest of fairness, they make public. Professors may also inform you personally of opportunities.

The weekly *Chronicle of Higher Education* lists job announcements both alphabetically by field and with larger "Bulletin Board" descriptions that are indexed by both geographical location and field. It is accessible on the Internet at "Academe This Week" (http:// chronicle.merit.edu/) and hard copies are available in the Office of Career Services Reading Room Annex. The Sunday *New York Times* also has academic job listings, as do some local papers.

Despite the structured formality of academic job listings, don't overlook the potential of networking to generate job leads. Several job seekers have heard about positions unexpectedly through networking contacts. For example, John Fox was called out of the blue about a tenure-track job in anthropology at Boston University's College of General Studies as a result of an informational interview (about academic administration) he had held with the Dean of the College several months earlier. The Dean recommended him to the department chairman, who called John for an interview even though they had a surfeit of formal applicants. Happily, he got the job. Another example is Allan Fung, a job candidate in HEAL who was about to take a nonacademic job in Hong Kong when he received a call from the chairman of the East Asian program at Brown inquiring if he would like to apply for a replacement position in Chinese history that had just opened up. He had met this professor several months earlier at a dinner party to which Allan had "tagged along" with a former adviser. Allan got the job.

Make a habit of keeping up-to-date on all sources of job listings. Because published job listings come out on an established timetable, unexpected openings may be listed in sources that publish more frequently, or they may depend upon individual mailings. Send your applications and dossier promptly, preferably well in advance of the deadline, although materials customarily will be accepted if postmarked by the deadline. If you are having difficulty completing your application materials, you should call and ask if a later date would be acceptable. If you are a chronic procrastinator, note that search committee members tend to expend the most time, effort, and enthusiasm on the early applicants.

Should you apply to schools that have not listed vacancies? Generally, this is a futile effort. The exception is when you have geographic constraints and need to find a position in a specific area. Then a letter to the chair of the relevant department, a follow-up call, and, if possible, a visit, can be fruitful, especially for replacement or part-time jobs.

Sometimes jobs are advertised in advance of actual approval for funding of the position. This is done with the expectation that by the time the recruiting season is over, the funding will be available. Of course, if the funding does not come through, both you, as a final candidate, and the department will be disappointed. However, you might be in a position to re-apply the following year if the job resurfaces.

Read the job description carefully, noting the type of appointment of each position (tenure-track, term appointment with possibility of tenure, term appointment renewable, or term appointment nonrenewable) and the qualifications required for it. Conventional advice is to limit your applications to jobs which interest you and for which you are genuinely qualified, but market conditions suggest a less selective strategy. Bear in mind that search committees do not always have a clear idea of what they want. This may be reflected in a very general job description, and/or by their ultimately appointing an impressive candidate whose field is totally out of the advertised specialty. It is better to apply widely and be rejected than to miss out on a possible opportunity, especially given that you can often tailor your qualifications to fit (at least adequately) a variety of job descriptions. On the other hand, use common sense to avoid outrageous fits as well as to gauge the added cost of your time.

In summary, this is a very taxing and stressful time. Try to resist the temptation to shortchange and/or procrastinate on some of the crucial preliminary steps, including preparing your credentials, the subject of the next chapter.

Chapter Four

Application Materials

Think of your application materials as the way to get from the application pile to the interview pile. Remember that academic search committees will only give your materials a quick review in the initial stages of the search process, as they look for reasons to eliminate people. You want your application—letter, c.v., reference letters, and any supplementary materials—to be clear, accurate, and compelling enough to win you, first, a careful look and, second, the coveted interview.

Examples of c.v.'s and cover letters are included here for you to use as guides; however, there is no substitute for crafting your own unique version of both. It is a good idea to ask your advisers, your colleagues, and the Ph.D. counselors at the Office of Career Services for critiques of your drafts. Items that may seem perfectly clear to you may not appear that way to a reader who does not know you. You owe it to yourself to get as much feedback as possible before you submit your application.

Establishing a Dossier and
Gathering Letters of Recommendation

Although letters of recommendation are extremely important, you have less control in this area than in some others. Therefore, it's important to do all you can to assure the best possible letters. First, if you have followed the advice in Chapter One, you have already collected letters of recommendation throughout your graduate program and updated them as you needed them for fellowships or jobs. For the job search you will need current letters from your thesis adviser and from two or more additional faculty members at Harvard or other institutions who know your work and/or who have supervised your teaching. The most helpful letters of reference discuss in enthusiastic *detail* what is special about your work and about you as a scholar and a person, so that you stand out as an individual in a pool of talented candidates.

Give some thought to who would write the strongest letters for you (this may vary according to the job) and solicit your adviser's opinion as well. In requesting letters from professors, you might ask if they would "feel comfortable" writing a strong letter for you. In addition, you can help them by giving them some of your written work, including the most recent version of your dissertation, and discussing with them your goals and aspirations, the highlights of your graduate program, special projects you have undertaken, and what you see as your particular strengths (or even any potential weaknesses they might be able to address convincingly). Professor James Alt of the Government Department asks his advisees to write up a page or two of paragraph-length "talking points" under the heading "Why I am better than sliced bread" to strengthen his verbal and written recommendations.

Since the preference in the academic world is for confidential letters, you will need a place to collect them. The Dossier Service at the Office of Career Services serves as a confidential repository for your letters and sends them out at your request. After you establish a file, you may add letters at any time and select which professors' letters you wish to have sent out, thus tailoring them to your application. Your file will be kept permanently and sent out at your request at any time during your professional life. If your department does not customarily use the Dossier Service, you still may want to establish a back-up file there. If you rely on the department, it is imperative that you keep track of whether your reference letters have been sent. In any case, it is the applicant's responsibility to ensure that references arrive on time.

While you will not be familiar with the contents of the letters, you probably will have some idea of which aspects of your professional preparation each recommender will address. For any job, you should probably include one letter that addresses your teaching skills, but if you are seeking a position in a "teaching college," try to include a letter from a professor who can *focus* on your teaching skills, as well as letters that mention them in passing. In selecting the letters to be forwarded, strive for a balanced representation in light of the particular job. When thinking about how many letters to send, you might recall Government Professor Sidney Verba's suggested "minimum winning coalition"—that is, it is better to have a few letters that you know are very strong recommendations than a larger number of letters which may include a mediocre recommendation, because the mediocre one might carry undue negative weight.

Schools may request that, along with your application, you send letters of recommendation or names of references pending further interest in your application. In either case, it is appropriate to request that your dossier be sent.

Preparing Your Curriculum Vitae and Dissertation Abstract

A curriculum vitae (c.v. or vita for short) differs from a résumé in that it is a summary document of your *educational and academic* history. It should be designed to present your accomplishments in the strongest way possible, consistent with honesty. Because its purpose is to outline your credentials for an academic position, any work experience that is not directly or indirectly relevant is customarily condensed or even omitted. It is frequently longer than a résumé, averaging two to four pages. It may include—usually as an addendum—additional information, such as a dissertation abstract and statements of teaching and research interests. You must have a c.v. for job applications, and you may need one earlier in graduate school to submit for fellowships or part-time positions such as House tutorships.

Your c.v. will evolve continually to reflect your additional experience and publications. For this reason, and because you may want to tailor it to the requirements of positions for which you will apply, you should produce your c.v. on your own computer, with your own word-processing package. In fact, a "canned" or "slick" look may be detrimental to your application. Your c.v. should be printed by a letter-quality printer on clean, high-quality white or off-white bond paper. If in doubt about two kinds of paper, it is always better to err on the side of conservatism.

Never underestimate the power of a legible and attractive format. A system of graphic hierarchy that organizes major and subcategories into easily recognized divisions enhances readability. Avoid dense blocks of information, which a reader may be inclined to skip. Use upper and lower case, boldface, and underlining to distinguish types of information. Use italics sparingly, reserving them for foreign phrases (e.g., *magna cum laude*) and the titles of books or journals; you might also want to use them for your dissertation title or to set off information such as course titles. Be consistent: the typeface you select for each category of heading should be used consistently throughout. Finally, at all costs, check and recheck your c.v. for grammatical, spelling, or typographical errors that might give readers an excuse to toss you into the "reject" pile. When you are finished, ask a friend and your advisers to look it over for any errors you might have missed.

Good organization is half the battle in presenting the content. How you organize the information tells the reader what you consider most important about yourself as a candidate for a particular job, so feel free to modify and rearrange the information and presentation depending on the type of job you are applying for. Typically, c.v.'s are organized in the following fashion:

Name and address. Your name should appear at the top of each page. On the first page, it should be distinguished by centering, boldface, upper-case letters, or a dividing line. It need not be as prominent on subsequent pages. Page numbers should appear on all pages except the first.

If you have both home and work addresses, list them at the top of the first page, with phone numbers and e-mail addresses where you can be reached during the day. (Since much academic communication is by telephone and, increasingly, by e-mail, it is essential to have an e-mail account or at least a telephone answering machine so that you are accessible during the entire job-search process.)

In order to present as professional a candidacy as possible, most applicants leave out personal information such as age, ethnic or national origin, religious affiliation, military service, or marital status. There are situations, however, where some of this information may enhance your candidacy, as for theological or language studies. Some applicants choose to include personal information for their own reasons, especially if the chronology of their work and educational history is confusing. This is an individual decision, and should be made thoughtfully. If you are a foreign scholar with U.S. citizenship or permanent resident status, it is to your advantage to include this information; if you are a resident alien, however, you may not want to call attention to your status.

Education. List your education in reverse chronological order, ending with college. High school is usually irrelevant. Include all the institutions you've attended, concentrations you've completed, and degrees you've received. If a degree is expected, indicate this by parentheses or by the words "degree expected . . . ," followed by the date you anticipate finishing. Be as honest as you can about your timetable for completion. You can lead either with the institution followed by the degree and the field, or with the degree; the date generally comes last. Using columns to present this information can be effective (see the samples at the end of this chapter).

Educational distinctions, such as honors and prizes, may appear in this section, but may also go into their own section. Honors accompanying the degree, e.g., *magna cum laude* or "with highest honors in . . . ," are presented as part of the degree. In some disciplines (e.g., history or economics), general exam fields or fields of specialization are included in this section either under the Ph.D. degree or after all the degrees. You also can group language study or special nondegree study separately.

Dissertation. First-time job seekers in the humanities and social sciences generally devote a separate section to the dissertation; this is the exception in the natural sciences. State the title of your dissertation and include the names of your advisers. A separate one- or two-page summary (try to keep it to one) is conventionally attached to the c.v., and this is indicated by a parenthetical note to "see attached summary (or abstract)." Alternatively, if you are just at the beginning of your dissertation research, or if you only need a streamlined version of your c.v., you could summarize the major points of your thesis in a brief, concise paragraph in this section. For some disciplines, such as English and anthropology, it is customary to include a thumbnail description. Natural scientists briefly describe their dissertation research under the heading of "Research Experience," though they may also include the title under the degree. They generally elaborate on their dissertation research in the "Statement of Research and Scholarly Interests" section. (See the discussion of supplementary materials on p. 51.)

From this point on you have more latitude in shaping the organization, so you should be guided by your strengths, the requirements of the particular type of jobs for which you are applying, and the conventions of your discipline.

Fellowships and Awards (or Fellowships and Honors). This section is a good place to list research-related and dissertation-support grants, fellowships, and awards that supplement any educational distinctions that you may have listed under "Education." Most candidates include all their honors and awards in this section. Do not overdo it, however; in general, don't include high-school honors (except for highly prestigious national awards) and minor college awards, especially if your list is extensive. This section often, but by no means always, comes near the top of the vita; indeed, many applicants who feel that their awards are not very significant, recent, or relevant, choose to place this category later in the c.v. or to omit it altogether as a section. If you have received an award that is not widely recognized or which is not self-explanatory, a descriptive note is recommended, e.g., "for dissertation research in Italy."

If you are a scientist or in another discipline for which you have applied and received research grants, you may want to create a separate "Grants" or "Research Grants" section. This would probably come later on in the vita.

Areas of Specialization. Other titles for this category are: "Areas of Research Interest," "Prepared to Teach," "Areas of Competence/Expertise," or "Principal Research and Teaching Interests." This is an optional section which succinctly lists your teaching and research strengths, interests, and competence. The advantage of including it is that it provides a brief overview of your skills; the disadvantage is that it may package you too neatly, and not allow for a wider interpretation of your qualifications. If you choose to include it, make your categories as broad as possible to cover a variety of teaching situations, but not so broad that you lose definition. In addition, follow discipline conventions about where to include it but don't give it undue space on the first page. All other things being equal, it's better to leave it for a cover letter, where you can tailor it closely to a particular position. However, check with your adviser and peers, because all other things are rarely equal.

Research Experience. Scientists tend to follow "Education" with this section, and candidates for jobs in research universities will probably put it first in their "Experience" categories (e.g., before "Teaching"). Scientists will briefly describe their postdoctoral, doctoral, and possibly undergraduate research, including both the substance and techniques employed, if relevant. Recent summer, intern, and interim research jobs are also customarily included. List the names of the institution and professor and/or project, with dates. Along with your descriptions, note any particular contribution you made, such as any resulting publications. Scientists and some others in strong research disciplines usually append a "Statement of Research Interests" as well. Anthropologists will have a section on "Field Research," including project names and locations, and a description of tasks and accomplishments, but this section generally comes after "Teaching Experience."

Teaching Experience. Where you place this section depends on the target institution as well as your strengths as a candidate; for example, you probably want to place it earlier if you are applying to a small teaching college. The basic information you want to convey is where, what, and when you have taught, and your titles.

This section can be organized in a number of different ways. For those who have taught in a variety of institutions, you might want to create two categories: "Positions Held" and "Courses Taught." Or you may want to lead with the name of the institution, followed by your title and department, and, finally, by your courses. In the more likely event that you have taught only at Harvard, you may want to categorize your experience by department (especially if you have taught in more than one department or Harvard school), your title (i.e., "Tutor," "Teaching Fellow," or "Instructor"), or names of courses.

How you arrange the information depends upon your individual history. If, for example, you have led courses both as a section leader or head section leader, and have also taught small tutorials, you may prefer to list your titles first. You will also want to describe your different functions and responsibilities, using active verbs, if possible, and avoiding repetition (e.g., describe what a section leader does only once). If a course title isn't self-explanatory, you may want to give a thumbnail description of it. With Harvard-specific information, leave out irrelevant data, such as course numbers, and be sure to clarify relevant information, such as the difference between being an instructor or a tutor versus a section leader. If you have taught in a wide variety of courses, you may choose to list the courses first, with your job titles later. Alternatively, block, italicize, or otherwise distinguish your course titles to help the reader to grasp quickly the variety of courses you have taught. Assuming your title and responsibilities were similar, list any given course only once, indicating the number of times you taught it by the dates.

Publications and Presentations. Where you place this section in your c.v. depends on the strength of your publication record. If it is substantial, you may decide that it comes first. However, if this section is quite lengthy, or conversely, not very substantive, it customarily comes at the end of a c.v. Scientists and all scholars past their first job put this section at the end. Some candidates subdivide this category into "Publications" and "Papers and Presentations" if they have enough to list under separate categories. They may further divide "Publications" into some combination of "Books," "Refereed Articles," "Abstracts," "Reviews," and/or "Other Publications" (a good category for a *limited* dose of popular, journalistic, or creative writing publications, or those from earlier jobs that are not relevant to your current field). Note that articles close to submission or pending a decision by a journal or publisher should be designated as "Papers," "Submitted Articles," or possibly "Works in Progress" (see below). The titles of your publications should be listed in standard bibliographic form, and you should include the dates and locations with the titles of your presentations.

Work in Progress. This is an optional category for listing articles or manuscripts that are relatively far along, perhaps close to submission. Articles or book manuscripts pending decision can be listed here or in the "Publications" section if they are clearly marked as "under review." This should be a short list and certainly should not exceed the length of the "Publications and Presentations" section.

Related Professional Experience. You can use this category to record any experience that is related to teaching, research, administration, academic service, or to your discipline or profession in general. This could include House-related activities, such as a resident or nonresident tutorship, committee work, editorial work, conference organizing, minor research assistantships, or other relevant work experience. In some fields, the relevant work experience is important enough to merit a separate section. Examples include "Curatorial or Museum Experience" for art historians or anthropologists; "Performance Experience" for music scholars; "Consulting or R&D Experience" for engineering or applied science candidates; "Editing, Translating, and Interpreting Experience" for comparative or foreign language and literature scholars; and "Government or Policy Experience" for political scientists, economists, or policy analysts (if it hasn't been included already under "Research Experience"). Other possible subsections include "Professional or Scholarly Activities," "University Service," and "Administrative Experience."

Languages. This is the place to list your language skills and degrees of competency, such as "native," "fluent," "proficient," "working knowledge," "reading only," or "some reading and speaking." Be honest—if you haven't used Spanish since high school or your last two-week vacation to Mexico, it is probably best to omit it.

Other. This category is optional, and may include such miscellaneous personal information as memberships in professional or scholarly associations, travel or study abroad, or personal interests and activities. Other than memberships, this information does not form a regular part of the academic c.v., but if you feel that some part of your personal history may be relevant and of potential interest, you should include it. You can also give more specific headings, such as "International Experience" or "Professional Memberships."

References. Because academics tend to operate within small, informal networks, the names of your references will convey significant information to most readers. Most job applicants list their academic references at the end of the c.v., with full names, titles, institutional addresses, telephone numbers, and e-mail addresses, if available. Three references are expected, but you may list more if you feel their evaluations would add significant information. However, be aware that by listing the references, you are publicly committing to them and you are depriving yourself of the opportunity to tailor them to particular institutions. If you list them, be sure they are references you want to use regardless of where you apply. Alternatively, you can create two different versions of your vita, or designate your references (or at least additional ones) in the cover letter. Make sure your references have copies of your c.v. and dissertation abstract and are prepared for phone calls and informal inquiries about your qualifications.

Dissertation Abstract. Even if you have not completed your dissertation, you will need to produce a reasonably conclusive one- to two-page (preferably one-) summary of your work. This is usually appended as a separate page at the end of your c.v., and is clipped or stapled together with the previous pages. Your description should be clear and concise, summarizing the content of your work, placing it within its scholarly context, and noting its contribution to the field. It should be comprehensible to people outside your field, but scholarly enough to engender interest from those who are familiar with your area of expertise. Natural scientists are more likely to present a summary of their research interests and/or abstracts from each of their papers, which would include the dissertation. In writing your abstract, remember to change the language from the future tense of your proposals to the present tense of a "completed" work, and to run it by your advisers and a professor not in your subfield. Examples are included at the end of this chapter, and you can also consult related dissertations in the Harvard Archives or *Dissertation Abstracts International* (in Widener Library) for style or format.

Preparing Supplementary Materials

In addition to your c.v. and letters of reference, you may be asked to submit a finished chapter of your dissertation or reprints of articles you have published. Occasionally you may be requested to forward course syllabi. Scientists, customarily, and nonscientists, occasionally, are asked to submit a "Statement of Research and Scholarly Interests." Often these supplementary materials are requested only after you make the initial cut. Send what is requested and honor any explicit limitations on materials; e.g., don't send writing samples if the job announcements say not to. In the absence of explicit directions, use common sense: you might add a reprint of an article or a concise summary of teaching evaluations or research interests, knowing that the worst that can happen is that they end up in the trash can.

Statement of Research and Scholarly Interests. As a graduate student you should have developed research interests that will sustain you after you have finished your dissertation and that are more ambitious than simply reworking your dissertation for publication. Nonscientists, if asked for this statement, will need to provide a one- or two-page statement of scholarly objectives for the near future, that is, the next two to five years. Scientists are expected to produce a two- to four-page statement of their research to date and their proposed postdoctoral research. In the "research to date" discussion, you will describe your thesis research methodology, lab skills, and substantive findings in some detail, but you may also include earlier undergraduate, summer, or other employment-related research experience. (If the application is for an assistant professorship, obviously you will include research projects for the upcoming few years only.) No matter what your discipline, keep your research goals realistic, focused, and suggestive of an exciting contribution to the field. Naturally, many of your ideas will be outgrowths of the research you have done for your dissertation, but you should be able to convey how you anticipate moving beyond your early research. One way to think about this is to consider what your next book might be about, or what proposal you would develop for a postdoctoral fellowship application.

Samples of Your Work. As noted earlier, avoid the temptation to weigh down your application with additional materials, unless you are specifically requested to do so. Be prepared, however, to send offprints of your published works and a good, representative chapter of your dissertation upon request. Try to keep the dissertation sample to about twenty-five pages and to make the first few pages compelling enough to keep the search committee members reading. If you send a partial dissertation chapter, be sure to write a lead-in and lead-out to provide context. It might be appropriate to include an offprint of a published article, but do not send unsolicited copies of seminar reports, conference presentations, or other unpublished works.

Teaching Materials. Teaching experience and ability seem to carry more weight now than previously, even in large research universities. As Harvard graduate students, particularly in the humanities and social sciences, you usually have extensive teaching experience that you can turn to your advantage in a competitive market. If you have developed a teaching portfolio (see p. 18), you already have a statement of your teaching philosophy, course descriptions and syllabi, and summaries of teaching evaluations and student comments, as well as the original records. You may even have teaching videos, which smaller teaching colleges sometimes request in lieu of preliminary interviews. Use your judgment about what to use at each stage. For your application to a teaching college, send anything requested in the job announcement, and consider sending an unsolicited summary evaluation sheet and/or a concise syllabus, especially if you designed it. You should bring these and other teaching materials to a preliminary or campus interview. For a particularly appealing job, you may even want to develop a rough syllabus of a course that you know you would teach if hired.

Course Lists or Transcripts. Very occasionally you will be asked to submit a list of your graduate courses or your transcript. You may choose to include a list of course work if it demonstrates breadth or competence in areas required by the position and not shown in your other work.

Writing Cover Letters

You make your first impression with your cover letter, and in some cases it may even determine whether or not the reader will bother to continue reading. Cover letters not only allow you a more personal forum than the c.v., but they also can and should be tailored individually to each job for which you apply. Disciplines vary in the importance accorded to cover letters (e.g., scientists and economists seem to weigh them less heavily), but it is safe to assume that it will take both time and effort to craft a compelling one. You will need to pay close attention to your style and tone as well as to the substance. Strive for a clear, concise, jargon-free, and graceful style, and a professional yet natural tone, which is neither self-effacing nor arrogant. Writing cover letters is challenging, but once you produce the first one the rest involve substantially less effort.

The cover letter gives you the opportunity to highlight and elaborate on points of interest from your c.v. that are particularly pertinent to the job description. You are not merely restating information presented elsewhere, but, rather, are demonstrating that your experience meets the department's stated needs. You can go into more detail about a relevant course, or explain more fully how your research area can make a contribution to a particular department. You also can make a case for qualifying for a position outside your apparent specialty, by emphasizing unusual or informal experience.

Before you begin to draft your letters, do some preliminary research on the department and school, and consider that information along with the job description. Try to get some sense of what they are seeking. Are they replacing someone? Creating a new position? Is this a multidisciplinary or joint position? How would someone with your background be able to make a contribution? Your letter will be much stronger if you demonstrate more than a generic interest in the department and make a compelling case for a match.

Your letter should be addressed to a specific person, probably to either the head of the search committee or the department chair. If their names are not provided in the job description, look them up in the course catalog or call the department secretary. If you absolutely cannot get the information, address it to the Members of the Search Committee. The first paragraph should state how you learned of the job; this is particularly important if a professor or colleague referred you to it. You then should describe your status as a Harvard Ph.D. candidate and indicate when you expect to complete your dissertation and/or receive the Ph.D. Alternatively, describe your status as a Ph.D. in a postdoctoral or other academic position.

The second paragraph usually presents a brief synopsis of your dissertation and its significance for the field. If you have moved well beyond your dissertation, then start with the most recent research project (e.g., a book). It helps to convey enough passion and excitement about your work to "make" the reader want to learn more. At some point you should indicate your next research project or projects, beyond publication of the dissertation; this often follows naturally from the description of the dissertation.

The middle portion of the letter should describe your research and teaching qualifications in light of their specific relevance to the job. Compose this section with reference to the job description and your notes on the department and institution. The order of this discussion will change somewhat depending on the importance accorded to teaching by the institution to which you are applying. You will want to highlight the distinctive features of your experience that make you an appropriate candidate. If you are applying for a position that calls for expertise in an area not directly related to your dissertation but which you are willing and qualified to teach, you should take special care to outline your experience and credentials in that area. If you have an obvious weakness, it's probably best to confront it directly, giving plausible reasons for how you can compensate.

In addition to noting courses you are prepared to teach, you might suggest new courses that you would be interested in developing. Some overlap in the courses you are prepared to teach and courses already offered by the department may be welcomed because you could provide coverage for professors who take a sabbatical.

Your concluding paragraph should note your enclosures, such as the c.v. and any other requested materials. If you know that the department will be conducting interviews at the annual meeting, be sure to indicate your plans for attending. You might also summarize here (or even earlier) why you are particularly interested in the position, if you can give genuine and substantive reasons—specific institutional features or personal reasons (e.g., family in this area, attended this or a similar college). This can be particularly persuasive at less "elite" and geographically desirable colleges, who may regard the motives of Harvard applicants skeptically.

Criteria for length vary substantially by discipline. Scientists and "hard" social scientists like economists favor brief, concise cover letters, while humanists and other social scientists tend to regard cover letters as another writing sample and are not troubled by letters over a page. As a general rule, however, keep it to one page, if possible, and to no more than a page and a half.

Should you use department letterhead? If you are employed as an instructor, it is certainly appropriate; the policy may be different if you are a teaching fellow, so be sure to discuss it with your department. If you have the option, using letterhead adds an attractive, professional aura to your letter.

Try to let the letter flow naturally and express something of your personality. One GSAS graduate now teaching English at a small liberal arts college calls this letting your own "voice" shine through. In other words, use the examples here as guides but not as templates! Keep in mind, however, one inviolable rule: make sure the letter is free of grammatical and typographical errors, and that it is clean and neat. And, of course, be sure to keep a copy for your records.

In summary, preparing your credentials can seem both tedious and daunting, and it is time-consuming at first. But the effort expended up-front will pay off—both immediately, in terms of increasing your job chances, and, down the line, in honing your self-presentation skills. You will undoubtedly tinker with your c.v. and basic cover letter as you gain experience on the market, but you will be surprised how easily you can "whip off" most cover letters after the initial batch.

Sample Application Materials

As previously noted, these sample vitas, dissertation abstracts, cover letters, and other application materials are presented as exactly that—sample, guides, and idea generators, but *not* as templates that can limit the presentation of your own unique credentials. While they are exemplary, they are not perfect, and they are chosen to represent a mix of disciplines, experience, career stages, and target institutions.

Names (both of applicants and letter recipients) and other obvious identifying characteristics like phone numbers have been changed, except in one case. It is important to remember that the small-page format of this book reduces the amount of material that can fit on a page as well as the size of the type (you would, of course, *never* use such small type!). It also can affect where the page breaks occur. Sometimes but not always, the original length of the c.v. or letter is noted in the commentary accompanying each example. Finally, in the interest of space, we have omitted or shortened some materials, such as references, some presentations, and nonacademic activities; the omissions are indicated in the c.v.'s.

A note about cover letter styles: included here are the two common formats for business letters, the left-block (everything is aligned to the left margin, including the first word of the paragraph) and the modified-block or standard (the return address and closing/signature begin right of center and paragraphs may or may not be indented).

The preference here has been to italicize publications and journals, etc., but underlining is still acceptable. Fonts and sizes are not varied as much as they would be in reality because of production constraints.

Materials are presented alphabetically by applicant within the three broad discipline categories—humanities, social sciences, and natural sciences.

P.O. Box 380000
Cambridge, MA 02238
(617) 493-0000
December 28, 1995

Dean Karen Wolff
Oberlin College Conservatory of Music
Oberlin, Ohio 44074

Dear Dean Wolff:

I write to apply for the positions in Music Theory. I am particularly interested in teaching at Oberlin because the college-conservatory environment will draw from my abilities as a theorist, teacher, and performer. Currently a graduate student in the Music Department at Harvard University, I plan to complete my doctorate by September 1996.

My dissertation developed from my desire—as a singer—to learn about Arnold Schoenberg's *Lieder* for voice and piano. I explore text-music relationships in a repertoire that has received scant attention. This investigation of Opp. 2, 3, and 6 applies Schenkerian analytical techniques to reveal tonal norms as well as chromatic extremes, building upon foundational studies by Proctor, Stein, Brown, and McCreless. Characteristics of *fin-de-siècle* chromaticism occur at all structural levels, pushing—and sometimes, exceeding—the conventions of tonal syntax. My research reveals that the poetry reflects onto the musical surface, as well as the middleground and background, exhibiting a wealth of correspondences between the text and music.

I see an inseparable link between research and teaching: the more I know, the more I have to offer my students. This fall, I taught a junior-level music analysis course at the University of Massachusetts in Amherst. As a Teaching Fellow at Harvard, I have taught sophomore theory and counterpoint, and I will teach 20th-century analytical techniques this spring. And at the University of North Texas, I had complete responsibility for all components of two first-year music theory courses. Thus, I am proficient in teaching the theory and analysis of music from the 18th through the 20th centuries. I particularly enjoy the challenge of increasing students' musicianship skills and would welcome an opportunity to develop an advanced ear training and sight singing course using 20th-century repertoire. In addition, I can offer courses on text-music relationships, Schoenberg, 19th-century chromaticism, and Schenkerian analysis.

Student response to my teaching is very positive, as indicated by representative remarks from evaluations:

> *YAY CHRISTINA!! excellent teaching ability—was able to impart not only complex knowledge but also a real enthusiasm—willingness above and beyond the call of duty to help individual students!*

> *I liked the course because of the teacher. She was hard, yet helped me improve my grade tremendously.*

very clear explanations
good choice of musical examples
always available to answer questions

As a lyric soprano, I perform regularly in solo and chamber recitals, as well as in larger concerts. In November, for example, I sang a recital that included Couperin's *Leçons de Ténèbres*. In September I performed selections from Wolf's *Italianisches Liederbuch* for the Harvard Music Department, and last June I performed the role of Belinda in *Dido and Aeneas*. My first love, however, is choral music. In Boston, I have sung with the professional choir at the Church of the Advent, and in the 1980s I sang four summer seasons with the Santa Fe Desert Chorale.

I have enclosed my c.v., and you will receive my dossier file under separate cover. Thank you for considering my application. I look forward to hearing from you.

Sincerely,

Christina I. Gutierrez

Commentary: It might have been better to append a summary sheet of teaching evaluations and comments rather than put them in the cover letter. In the c.v., Christina Gutierrez elects to put dates in the margins; she manages this effectively by blocking the more substantive material. In fact, it may even be preferable to highlight the chronology in the requisite "Performance" section. The "Presentations" section might have followed "Teaching Experience," especially for a teaching college such as Oberlin. Although she did not get the Oberlin job, Gutierrez received an excellent tenure-track assistant professor position at the University of Texas at Austin.

CHRISTINA ISABELA GUTIERREZ
PO Box 380000
Cambridge, MA 02238
(617) 493-0000
Fax: (617) 496-0000
gutierrez @ fas.harvard.edu

EDUCATION

Ph.D.	Harvard University	Music Theory	(1996)
A.M.	Harvard University	Music Theory	1993
M.M.	University of North Texas	Music Theory	1990
B.M.	University of North Texas	Music Education	1982

DISSERTATION

"Text-Music Relationships in Arnold Schoenberg's Tonal Lieder for Voice and Piano." Adviser: David Lewin, Walter W. Naumburg Professor of Music

PRESENTATIONS

"Musical Representation of Manifest and Latent Thoughts in Arnold Schoenberg's
Lieder: 'Mädchenlied' Op. 6 no. 3 and 'Traumleben' Op. 6 no. 1"
New England Conference of Music Theorists—April 8, 1995

"Tonality, Chromaticism, and Text-Music Relationships in Arnold Schoenberg's
Op. 6 no. 2 'Alles' and Op. 6 no. 3 'Madchenlied'"
University of North Texas—March 24, 1994
West Coast Conference of Music Theory and Analysis—March 26, 1994

FELLOWSHIPS AND AWARDS

1995	Distinction in Teaching Award, Harvard University
1994	Graduate Society Fellowship for Dissertation Research, Harvard
1994	John Knowles Paine Traveling Fellowship (to Arnold Schoenberg Institute), Harvard University
1990-present	Graduate Prize Fellowship, Harvard University
1990-94	Ford Foundation Pre-Doctoral Fellowship
1990	Dorothy Danforth Fellowship (declined)
1990	CIC Fellowship (declined)
1990	UNT Pi Kappa Lambda Masters Class Award
1982	NTSU Outstanding Student in Choral Music Education
1982	Pi Kappa Lambda
1981	Mortar Board

TEACHING EXPERIENCE

University of Massachusetts, Amherst, MA
Fall 1995   *Lecturer, Music Theory*
                 Teach junior-level analysis course.

Harvard University, Cambridge, MA
Spring 1996   *Teaching Fellow*, Analysis of 20th-Century Music

TEACHING EXPERIENCE (Continued)

<u>Harvard University</u>, Cambridge, MA

1994-95	*Teaching Fellow,* Sophomore Music Theory
	Instruct and grade keyboard exercises and lead weekly one-hour sections to reinforce ear training, part writing and analysis skills; grade homework and tests.
1992-93	*Teaching Fellow,* Counterpoint (16th- and 18th-century styles)
	Lead weekly one-hour sections to survey relevant repertoire and address student questions.

<u>University of North Texas</u>, Denton, TX

1989-90	*Teaching Fellow,* Freshman Theory
	Complete responsibility for creating syllabi and teaching two classes, including exercises in analysis and part writing, ear training, sight singing, and keyboard skills.

<u>Dallas, Texas</u>   CIG Sight Singing Clinics

1989-93	Organized and taught one-week classes for junior and senior high school choir students.

<u>Louisiana School for Math, Science and the Arts</u>, Natchitoches, LA

1988-89	*Faculty Member in Dept. of Creative and Performing Arts*
	Taught 15 students in applied voice, one class in music theory, and conducted two choirs. Voice students won regional NATS Auditions.

<u>McAllen Independent School District</u>, McAllen, TX

1984-87	*Junior High Choir Director*

<u>The Selwyn School</u>, Denton, TX

1982-84	*K-12 Music Director and Head of Fine Arts Department*

RELATED PROFESSIONAL EXPERIENCE

Fall 1991-present	*Resident Music Tutor* at Mather House, Harvard University Advise undergraduates on academic and nonacademic issues, coordinate musical activities; oversee use and care of music facilities; coach vocal ensembles in Mather Chamber Music program; organize events to welcome new residents.
Sept. 1995	"An Introduction to Undergraduate House Life." Workshop for Teaching in English Program, Derek Bok Center for Teaching
Sept. 1994-Jan. 1995	"Tips for New Teachers." Workshop for Teaching Orientation, Bok Center
Fall 1993	Discussion Leadership Seminar participant, Bok Center
1991-94	Editorial Assistant, Music Theory On-line Journal
Summers '85, '86, '89	Company Manager, Santa Fe Desert Chorale

VOCAL AND CHORAL PERFORMANCE

Jan. 1996	King's Chapel Noon Recital Series, Boston, MA
Nov. 1995	Early Music at Mather Recital Series, Harvard University Soprano duets by Monteverdi, Handel, and Couperin
Sept. 1995	Harvard University Department of Music Selections from *Wolf's Italianisches Leiderbuch*
June 1995	Early Music at Harvard (concurrent with Boston Early Music Festival) Belinda in Purcell's *Dido and Aeneas* Couperin's *Leçons de Ténèbres*
May 1994	*Lieder* Recital Songs of Schubert, Brahms, Wolf, Strauss, and Schoenberg
Feb. 1993	Vox Baleanarum (Harvard's Cello Choir) Soloist: Villa-Lobos's *Bachianas Brasileiras #5*
1992-93	Church of the Advent, Boston, MA Soprano in Professional Choir and occasional soloist and cantor
1990-92	Harvard University Choir and daily Morning Choir Soloist: Allegri's "Miserere," Handel's *Messiah* Part III, Faure's *Requiem*, Beach's "Let This Mind Be in You" (Released on: Northeastern Classical Arts NR 247-CD)
Summers '88, '86, '85, '83	Santa Fe Desert Chorale, Santa Fe, NM Soprano Section Leader and Soloist in Professional Choir
1983-84	Denton Bach Society, Denton, TX
1987-88	Soloist: J.S. Bach Cantata # 1
1985-87	Valley Symphony Chorale, Edinburg, TX Soloist: Stravinsky *Mass*

UNIVERSITY AND COMMUNITY SERVICE

Presently	Professional Development Committee Member, Society of Music Theory
1992-93	Student Colloquium Committee, Music Theory Representative
Fall 1992	Recruiter for Graduate School of Arts and Sciences
1992	Nominating Committee Member, New England Conference of Music Theorists
1991-92	Group for Gender Studies in Music, Treasurer

November 28, 1989

Professor Terrance Smith
Acting Chair
German Department
University of California
Irvine, CA 92717

Dear Professor Smith:

I am writing to apply for the position in German advertised by your department. I was excited to learn of this opportunity, since U.C. Irvine is the type of school at which I would like most to teach: a dynamic institution in which both quality teaching and individual scholarship are important. I am a Ph.D. candidate in Comparative Literature at Harvard University; my major field is German. I have had solid preparation in all periods of German literature; my main interests are in twentieth-century fiction, but I am also very interested in other periods and genres. My article on Goethe's *Wilhelm Meisters Lehrjahre*, for example, is being published next year in *Seminar*. I plan to complete my dissertation this spring and will be available to begin teaching by July 1, 1990.

As the enclosed summary indicates, my dissertation is an exploration of second person fiction, a phenomenon unaccounted for in previous narratological studies. I propose the term "narrative apostrophe" to describe instances in which the sender and receiver do not exist in the same circuit of communication, either ontologically, because one person is dead or absent, as in traditional apostrophe, or narratologically, because one exists in the discourse and the other outside it, as in traditional reader address by the narrator. The apostrophic gesture functions as an invitation to the actual reader—at least on a subliminal level—even when s/he can deduce that the communication is directed to someone else. My dissertation explores the ambiguities created by this double tug of identification using examples from the postwar German literary tradition, e.g., Günter Grass's *Katz und Maus*, Ilse Aichinger's "Spiegelgeschichte," and Christa Wolf's "Selbstversuch." Other texts I discuss range in period from the medieval to contemporary and in national literary tradition from French, Italian, American, and Modern Greek to Latin American.

As a graduate student at Harvard, I have had the privilege of teaching a wide variety of courses, including German language and literature courses. I have taught a two-semester small group tutorial which serves as an introduction to literary theory for Harvard's literature majors. The two syllabi I developed are enclosed. When I taught this course I had great success in incorporating German texts. Additionally, I have assisted in several interdisciplinary courses, for example, in a course on German culture and society in the Weimar and Nazi periods and in a course on the Holocaust and the phenomenon of genocide.

My future research and teaching interests continue in this direction; after I complete my dissertation, I would like to explore literary representations of the Holocaust, particularly German, but with a comparative component. I would also like to expand some preliminary work I have done on the German novella, especially in comparison to the development of the short story form in the Postwar period.

Please let me know if you would like me to furnish you with a sample of my written work or any other information. I can be contacted by telephone at (617) 863-0000. I will be attending the MLA convention in Washington, D.C. and will be available for an interview at any time except Friday morning, Dec. 29, when I will present my work on residual orality in Modern Greek prose fiction. I have asked the Dossier Service of Harvard University to send my letters of reference directly to you.

Thank you for considering my application.

Sincerely,

Imelda Konstantin

Commentary: On 8 1/2 × 11 paper, the letter was one page and the c.v. three pages long. Note the emphasis both on German language and literature (and de-emphasis of comparative literature and modern Greek) for this German Department job. Imelda Konstantin emphasizes her teaching experience because it is her strength, and because teaching is important for language jobs even in research universities. The first-paragraph reference to Irvine is too generic to be compelling (and, in fact, she did not get the Irvine job, but she did accept an offer from University of Texas at Austin).

CURRICULUM VITAE
Imelda Konstantin
180 Williams St. #1
Cambridge, MA 02138
(617) 863-0000

EDUCATION:

Harvard University, Ph.D., Comparative Literature *Fields*: German, Modern Greek, English. *Specializations*: nineteenth- and twentieth-century fiction, narratology, reader-response criticism, intertextuality, feminism	(expected) June 1990
Harvard University, A.M., Comparative Literature	November 1984
Aristotle University, Thessaloniki, Greece, Modern Greek Literature	1981-82
Harvard-Radcliffe College, A.B. *magna cum laude*, History and Literature	1981
Freie Universität, West Berlin, Germanistik	1978-79

DISSERTATION:

"Narrative Apostrophe: Case Studies in Second Person Fiction" (summary attached)
Advisers: Professors Dorrit Cohn and Judith Ryan

TEACHING EXPERIENCE (all at Harvard University):

<u>Instructor</u>, 1989-Present.

<u>Teaching Fellow</u>, 1984-89.

Language Instruction:

Elementary German, Harvard Extension School, 1989-90.

German for Reading Knowledge (mainly graduate students), Teaching Assistant, Spring 1988.

Elementary German (mainly undergraduates), 1987-88.

Elementary Modern Greek, Harvard Extension School, 1985-88.

Literature and Interdisciplinary Courses:

"Culture and Society: From Weimar to Nazi Germany" (Prof. Richard Hunt), Spring, Fall 1989

"Author, Reader, Text: Confrontations and Crises in Contemporary Literary Theory" (Prof. Susan R. Suleiman), Fall 1989, Spring 1987

TEACHING EXPERIENCE (continued):

Junior individual tutorial, Literature program (topics: Kleist; ethnic, especially Puerto Rican, literature; minor literature in a major discourse), 1989-90

"Explaining the Holocaust and the Phenomenon of Genocide" (Prof. Erich Goldhagen), Spring 1989

German Department Seniors' Colloquium: Presentation and guided discussion of Chamisso's *Peter Schlemihl* (1987), Lessing's *Nathan der Weise* (1988), and Günter Grass's *Katz und Maus* (1989)

Sophomore group tutorial, Literature program: "Introduction to Literary Theory" (see two attached syllabi which I developed), 1986-87

Junior individual tutorial, History and Literature: Survey of German Drama, 1986

"Modern [Anglo-American] Poetry" (Prof. Seamus Heaney), Spring 1985

"Comedy and the Novel" (Prof. Donald Fanger), Fall 1984

"The Burden of the Past and the Modern Greek Poet" (Prof. George P. Savidis), Spring 1984

PUBLICATIONS:

"Re-presentations of Time in *Wilhelm Meisters Lehrjahre*." *Seminar: A Journal of Germanic Studies*, forthcoming early 1990

SCHOLARLY PRESENTATIONS:

"Translation and the Anonymous 'You,'" Modern Language Association convention, Washington, DC, Dec. 29, 1989

"The Power of the Spoken Wor(l)d: "'I' and 'You' in Modern Greek Narrative," Modern Greek Studies Association (MGSA) Symposium, Minneapolis, MN, Oct. 1989

"Rhetorical Resuscitation: Apostrophe in Günter Grass's *Katz und Maus*," Society for the Study of Narrative Literature (SSNL) International Conference, Madison, WI, April 1989

"Teaching the Literature of a Foreign Culture," Harvard-Danforth Center for Teaching and Learning, Winter Orientation, Jan. 1989

"'Additionsfehler'? Nein! Re-presentations of Time in *Wilhelm Meisters Lehrjahre*," German Dept., Harvard University, and SSNL Conference on Narrative Literature, Columbus, OH, March, April 1988

"Sea and Self in Selected Prose Works of Alexandros Papadiamantis," MGSA Symposium, Providence, RI, Nov. 1987

"Toward an Intertextual Analysis of Alfred Döblin's *Berlin Alexanderplatz*: A Typology of Intertextual Transformations of the Bible," Germanic Circle and Comparative Literature Colloquium, Harvard University, Spring 1984

AWARDS:

Fellowship, *Hochschulferienkurs*, Weimar, GDR, Summer 1988

Jack M. Stein Teaching Prize, German Dept., Harvard University, May 1988

Two Commendations, Excellence in Teaching, Danforth Center for Teaching and Learning, Harvard University, 1987, 1988

Merit Fellow, Graduate School of Arts and Sciences (GSAS), Harvard University, 1985-86

Bernhard Blume Prize, German Dept., Harvard University, May 1984

I.H. Levin Scholarship, GSAS, Harvard University, 1983-84

Umberto Eco Prize, best essay in pro-seminar, Comparative Literature Dept., Harvard University, 1983

Fulbright Full Grant (study in Greece), 1981-82

Phi Beta Kappa, Radcliffe Iota Chapter, 1980

RELATED PROFESSIONAL EXPERIENCE:

Hochschulferienkurs, Weimar, GDR, gave seminar on my method of foreign language instruction, August 1988

Peer Teaching Consultant, Danforth Center for Teaching and Learning, 1988-Present

Non-Resident Tutor, North House (undergraduate residence). Advise students, organize and run German and Modern Greek Language Tables, 1984-Present

Volunteer Tutor, Cambridge Public Schools. Worked with Greek immigrant children to help make adjustment to the English language classroom, 1982-84

CERTIFICATIONS AND MEMBERSHIPS:

Basic, Advanced Certification, Rassias Method of Language Teaching, June 1986, Feb. 1988

Member, Society for the Study of Narrative Literature, 1988-Present

Member, American Association of Teachers of German, 1987-Present

Member, Modern Language Association, 1987-Present

Member, American Comparative Literature Association, 1985-Present

Member, Modern Greek Studies Association, 1979-Present

LANGUAGES: German, Modern Greek, French, Spanish, Classical and Koine Greek

Academic and teaching references available on request

Dissertation Summary
Imelda Konstantin

NARRATIVE APOSTROPHE: CASE STUDIES IN SECOND PERSON FICTION

In this dissertation I analyze uses of the second person in fiction other than dialogue. The feature that defines my corpus of texts is an incomplete circuit of communication. I borrow and extend the rhetorical term "apostrophe" to describe situations in which sender and receiver are not on the same plane (ontologically or narratologically), and therefore cannot talk or listen directly, or perhaps not at all, to one another. My examples include the familiar, often formulaic, reader addresses of the traditional novel and its modern parodies; apostrophes from one character to an absent other, from narrator to character, or even from character to narrator; rhetorical statements and questions; as well as a small corpus of modern fictional works which are narrated predominantly or exclusively in the second person. Although the latter are few in number, their existence challenges us to expand the theoretical framework of narratology in which a primary criterion for classification, person, has only two slots: first and third.

Drawing on philosophy, psychology, rhetoric, and linguistics, I argue that the second person pronoun extends an irretractable invitation to the listener. As readers, we have been trained to ignore this relational imperative by the presence of quotation marks, such as in quoted dialogue. But narrative apostrophes have no such boundaries, and therefore the reader potentially feels him/herself addressed, even when s/he can deduce the presence of another addressee. I document precisely this phenomenon in my opening chapter, "'Qui êtes-vous?' Reading Critics Reading Michel Butor's *La Modification*." Sophisticated French readers interpret Butor's "vous" as referring simultaneously to themselves and to Delmont, the protagonist. They do so, I argue, not only because of the psychological impact of the pronoun of narration, but also because of their experience of its historical use as the pronoun of reader address. I offer this point as a corrective to Morrissette's study of second person narration (1965), in which he locates antecedents for "narrative you" in the modern lyric, while ignoring the more obvious experience of previous uses in prose fiction. In the second chapter of my thesis, I propose a typology of second person fiction texts organized by the hermeneutical criterion of how the reader interprets the primary identity of the second person pronoun. The third chapter continues to explore the role of the reader/audience through a discussion of the inscription of storytelling in Modern Greek prose. The high level of residual orality which characterizes Modern Greek society, is particularly marked in its prose, I argue, by the ubiquitous presence of second person phrases such as "you say" and "you see."

In the second part of my thesis I explore the dynamics of the apostrophic gesture with regard to thematic issues of power and control. By apostrophizing, one exercises power by creating an other. But the same gesture, the lending of one's voice, also allows the other to become a subject, the "you" to become an "I." Thus the apostrophizer potentially loses control. In a close reading of Günter Grass's *Katz und Maus*, for example, I develop a new interpretation of the problematic relationship of Pilenz and Mahlke by exploring Pilenz's alternation between epic narration and apostrophe. In the penultimate chapter I explore similar issues of power and control as they are waged in the gender battle through close readings of Lillian Smith's *Strange Fruit*, Ilse Aichinger's "Spiegelgeschichte," and Italo Calvino's *If on a winter's night a traveler.* My final chapter considers the future of the pure second person form and its relation to popular literature, especially the fantastic, crime novels, and science fiction. I offer readings of Otto Walter's *Der Stumme*, Carlos Fuentes's *Aura*, and Jay McInerney's *Bright Lights, Big City.*

Through an exploration of these various issues, my dissertation does not argue for a coherent, unitary theory, but rather demonstrates the profound ambiguity of second person narration.

[The syllabi and writing assignments for "Introduction to Literary Theory" appended in the original are omitted here for space reasons.]

Dr. Sarah Kurtz
00 Waring Street
Belmont, MA 02178
(617) 484-0000

Professor Edward Chester
General Education History Search Committee
Office of Professional Education Division
Berklee College of Music
Boston, MA 02215
January 30, 1996

Dear Professor Chester:

I am delighted to learn of your search for a historian for Berklee. It is one of the institutions in the Boston area that has enriched my life personally over the years and it would be a privilege to be part of it. My friend, Bill Sagan, who teaches skat singing at the College, speaks about his experiences there with a certain passion that never fails to pique my interest in the place.

My training provides me with unconventional but intense preparation for teaching Western Civilization and non-European history at Berklee. My undergraduate concentration in Fine Arts combined loves for history and art to illuminate the evolution of Western Civilization in wonderful ways. Those were the days one could don backpack and hiking boots and hitchhike through European history via its churches, museums, fortresses, and mountains. As I crisscrossed the continent, the Mediterranean, the Middle East, and parts of Africa, Western Civilization came alive for me in ways that permanently infused my perceptions of self, society, and social change.

The Middle East became my home for the better part of a decade, and I founded a network for Arabs and Jews based in Jerusalem before these kinds of opportunities existed. Hundreds of individuals came to have first-time contact with the forbidden "other." The work spanned workshops throughout Israel, West Bank, and Gaza; meetings for reconciliation in Cyprus, Egypt, and Germany; and performance in an Arab-Jewish street theater group. During those years, I commuted to Europe to lead workshops for educators on nationalism, ethnicity, and religion. One of the most memorable experiences during those years was my stay in a convent (every Jewish girl's dream) in Belfast working with Catholic, Protestant, and British organizers.

This work eventually precipitated the questions which lured me back to the university where I took an interdisciplinary master's in Middle East Studies and then a doctorate in History and the Middle East with a research focus on women and gender. The graduate years afforded me an exceptional opportunity to teach a range of topics beyond the borders of my field including European (with Stanley Hoffmann and David Landes) and American (with Ellen Fitzpatrick) histories. My Western field of study for general exams was in modern American history (with

Stephen Thernstrom). Emphasis on Middle Eastern studies in my academic training enabled me to cultivate non-Eurocentric perspectives on diverse cultures and to bring a unique perspective to the teaching of Western Civilization.

My interest in curriculum development is long-standing. In eight years of teaching undergraduate courses, I designed six courses. An outstanding teaching experience in this arena was the three-year appointment to create and teach year-long history seminars for undergraduates which included curricula for the ancient, medieval, and modern periods. When I accepted a one-year appointment as visiting lecturer at Tufts University, I put together curricula for two courses in medieval and modern history and then synthesized the two to teach one course at Harvard.

My teaching experience spans not only a diversity of subject matter but educational contexts as well. I have taught in other countries, in other languages, undergraduates, graduates, adults who never went to college, high school students, classes of men only, in the university and in the community. I love teaching and have had the privilege of learning from students of incredibly diverse backgrounds. I have co-founded and administered new programs, participated in outreach programs that connected the university to the community, and in general, worked to expand cross-cultural and interdisciplinary connections.

I am particularly attracted to Berklee for its artistic and international student body. Just as music is an international language with rigorous and sensual, nitty-gritty and inspirational aspects that fosters understanding, so is history. Both art and history plumb basic questions of existence, contradiction, and consequence. The study of history, the exposure to other times and cultures, can subtly affect the production of art in conscious and unconscious ways. It would be an honor for me to become part of this project of exploration and excellence that seems to me to be Berklee.

Good luck in your search. I look forward to meeting you.

Sincerely,

Sarah Kurtz

Commentary: Sarah Kurtz's letter and the accompanying c.v. exemplify tailoring to a particular job—in this case, to an unconventional teaching institution, where history is part of general education requirements for degrees in music. Hence, in her c.v., she separates and highlights the relevant CORE courses she taught at Harvard, and she puts her "Fields of Study" at the end, since they don't quite fit the announcement. Highlighting course names in italics may be less effective than usual because she also italicizes publications on page 2. The letter stresses the diversity of her teaching experience, in terms of subject matter, students, educational contexts, and curriculum development; it also explains how this experience will enhance her teaching of Western Civilization, which, in fact, she had never taught. By tying in her own background with Berklee's mission and speaking in her own "voice," she leaves the reader with a memorable impression of her. The closing is on the informal side, but she got the job.

Sarah Helen Kurtz

00 Waring Street
Belmont, MA 02178
(617) 484-0000

Education	HARVARD UNIVERSITY, **Ph.D.** Nov. 1993 Joint Degree: History and Middle East Studies
	HARVARD UNIVERSITY, **M.A.** 1987 Middle East Studies
	BRANDEIS UNIVERSITY, **B.A.** Fine Arts, *magna cum laude*
Current Position	Affiliate in Research, Center for Middle East Studies, Harvard University, 1994-1996
Dissertation	*Founding and Confounding the Boundaries: Women and Gender in Jewish and Palestinian Nationalisms before 1950*

Teaching

Harvard University, <u>Teaching Fellow</u>   Spring and Fall 1994

Europe	*Development and Underdevelopment: The Historical Origins of the Inequality of Nations* CORE CURRICULUM (Professor David Landes)
Europe	*International Conflicts in the Modern World* CORE CURRICULUM (Professor Stanley Hoffmann)
Mideast	*Making and Remaking of the Modern Middle East* CORE CURRICULUM (Professor Roger Owen)

Tufts University, <u>Visiting Lecturer</u>, History   1992-93

Ancient and Medieval	*Issues of Gender in Islamic Societies* Created and taught new course on pre-modern Islamic historical, political, and cultural developments as they shaped roles of, and attitudes towards, men and women.
Modern	*History of Women in the Modern Middle East* Created and taught new course on 19th- and 20th-century history, politics, and culture.

Harvard University

<u>Lecturer</u>	*Middle East Studies/Sociology* *Women in Middle Eastern and Islamic Societies* Created new course on women in social and historical perspectives.	1993

Harvard University (continued)

Lecturer	*Tutorial: The History of the Middle East* Created new courses and taught undergraduate year-long seminars in medieval and modern periods.	1989-92
Teaching Fellow	*Society and Politics of 20th c. American History* History Department, Ellen Fitzpatrick *History of Palestine, Zionism and Israel* History Department, Zachary Lockman	1989
	Religion and Culture of Islam CORE CURRICULUM (William Graham and Ali Asani)	1988
	Thought and Change in the Middle East CORE CURRICULUM (Nur Yalman)	1986

Publications   "*Adam* and *Adama*, '*Ird* and *Ard:*' En-gendering Political Conflict and Identity," in *Gender and Power in the Middle East,* ed. Deniz Kandiyoti, I.B. Taurus, 1996.

Palestinian Women: Identity and Experience, Ebba Augustin, ed., review for *International Journal of Middle East Studies*, August 1995.

"Speaking the Unspoken," review of *An American Feminist in Palestine: The Intifada Years*, by Sherna Berger Gluck, for *Association of Middle Eastern Women's Studies Newsletter*, vol. X, no. 2 (May 1995).

"'Beyond the Veil' of Ignorance: Images of Middle Eastern Women in Two New High School Texts," review of *Women in Society: Israel* by Beth Uval and *Women in Society: Egypt* by Angele Samaan, *Lilith*, 18/4, pp. 30-31.

"A House Divided: Jerusalem and the Arab-Jewish Conflict," Review of Romann's and Weingrod's *Living Together Separately: Arabs and Jews in Contemporary Jerusalem, Harvard International Review* (Fall 1991): 61-64.

Presentations   "Histories of the Palestinian-Israeli Conflict," Community Education Seminars, Sudbury, Fall 1995.

"19th- and 20th-Century European and Middle Eastern National Movements: Role of the Balkans," Community Education Seminars, Sudbury, Fall 1995.

"Israel in the Middle East," Community Education Seminars, Sudbury, Spring 1995.

"Civilizing Women: Gender, Nation and Modernization in Palestine and Israel," Middle East Studies Association Annual Meeting, November 1994.

[Seven others included in the original are omitted here.]

Awards   U.S. Department of Education Pre-doctoral Research Award
                      1993
                      Foreign Language and Area Scholarship Award
                      Summer 1985 and academic year 1986-1987
                      Harvard University Scholarship Award
                      1985-1986
                      1984-1985

Professional   American Historical Association
Affiliations   Association of Middle Eastern Women's Studies
                      Middle East Studies Association
                      National Council for Research on Women

Administration/   *Middle East Journal*, 1996. Reviewer of article for
Outreach   publication.

                      Bunting Institute, 1995. Reviewer of postdoctoral fellowship
                      applications.

                      Committee for the Study of Women and Gender in Middle
                      Eastern and Islamic Societies, CMES, 1991-1994. Co-
                      founding member of a women's studies committee in Middle
                      East Studies at Harvard. Organizer of monthly forums and
                      creator of course on Middle East women.

                      Teaching Resource Center, Harvard, National Conference for
                      Educators: "The Role of Women and Girls in the Middle
                      East," July 6-9, 1993. Consultant to director, Carol Shedd, for
                      planning of conference. Also presented two papers.

                      Committee for Planning of Women's History Week, 1990-
                      1993. Helped organize and administer intensive weeklong
                      events, bringing scholars from around the country to
                      Cambridge.

                      *Passion for Life: Jewish and Palestinian Women's Folk Arts
                      and Oral Histories.* Spring 1989. Consultant to director of
                      exhibit co-sponsored by Oral History and Cambridge Multi-
                      Cultural Centers; co-led workshop with Palestinian woman for
                      community educators on history of Arabs and Jews.

                      Outreach Program, CMES, Harvard, Spring 1985. Cambridge
                      Rindge and Latin High School: Co-led two workshops for 400
                      pupils on Arab-Jewish relations and on Israeli-Palestinian
                      conflict for Middle East Week.

Related   Multigenerational Community Education Seminars
Professional   Director, Sudbury, MA, 1994-96.
Experience   Created curriculum, taught, and administered humanities
                      seminars for adults and high-school students on history,
                      religion, and the arts.

Related
Professional
Experience
(continued)

Intercultural Relations Program
Kennedy School of Government, Harvard, 1991-92.
Worked with Educational Fellows at Institute for Social and
Economic Policy in the Middle East. Led workshops for
Israeli, Palestinian, Jordanian, and Egyptian doctors and
healthcare professionals to constructively confront differences
and forge commitments across political barriers.

Research Assistant to Simcha Flapan, 1985.
CMES, Harvard University. Contributed to *The Birth of
Israel: Myths and Realities* (Pantheon, 1987).

Intercultural Relations Consultant, 1980-84.
Berkeley, CA. Planned and led conferences on the humanities:
history, religion, the arts.

Founder and Director of Network for Arab-Jewish
Communication in Jerusalem, 1973-80.
Worked with Jews and Arabs in Israel to create opportunities
for dialogue on nationalism, gender, race, religion, class.
Participated in Middle East conferences and meetings in
Cyprus, Germany, and Egypt. Led seminars for leaders
involved in Arab-Jewish work. Commuted to Europe to lead
seminars on nationalism, gender, class, and race in Belfast,
Dublin, London, Paris, Amsterdam, Stockholm, Copenhagen,
Athens, and Florence.

Fields of Study

Modern History with Zachary Lockman (Middle East)
Medieval History with Roy Mottahedeh (Islamic)
Modern American History with Stephen Thernstrom (social)

References

[Eight references included in the original are omitted here.]

000 K Street, #4-0
Boston, MA 02000
November 27, 1995

Professor Jason Winter
Chair
Department of History
Williams College
Williamstown, MA 01267

Dear Dr. Winter:

I am writing to apply for the position in Chinese History advertised in the Association of Asian Studies *Newsletter*. I am currently writing a dissertation at Harvard University under the direction of Professor Philip Kuhn, entitled "The Power of Mercy: The Early History of the Chinese Red Cross Society, 1900-1937." I will complete my dissertation in August 1996. An abbreviated version of my first chapter will be published this spring in *Papers on Chinese History* (Harvard University).

My research focuses on state-society relations in China in the early twentieth century. My dissertation, "The Power of Mercy," reveals changing patterns of elite participation in public affairs in late Qing and Republican China by examining the transformation of Chinese philanthropy from a sporadic local initiative, led by elites, to a sustained national effort, engaging a steadily growing segment of the Chinese polity. I use the archives of the Chinese Red Cross Society, as well as other published and unpublished materials gathered in China, Taiwan, Switzerland, and the U.S., to chart this shift in elite activity from the local to the national arena and to map out a parallel transition in elite self-definition. China's merchant and educated elite, caught in the flux of a crumbling dynastic system and an onslaught of foreign influences, used philanthropy, particularly the medical philanthropy espoused by the Chinese Red Cross, to create a social niche for themselves that was at once traditionally sanctioned and, at the same time, appealingly "modern." My study links these trends to China's growing nationalism and emerging interest in becoming a member of the international community. This investigation into the politics of humanitarianism places China's present-day engagement in the global arena in historical perspective and uncovers some of the earliest bases for the dissonance between China's international behavior and Western expectations for that behavior.

My work on the Chinese Red Cross Society also contributes to current scholarship on the rise of "civil society" in developing nations, an issue of central importance in today's era of emerging democracies. My research reveals the growth of alternative loci of power in the realm of social welfare action in China, power sources developed in a notably *non-confrontational*, mutually beneficial relationship with the state. These findings challenge much recent work on "civil society" which claims that the public sphere must operate in opposition to the state; they underscore the need to re-examine how social actors and governments work together. This in-depth study of philanthropic development in China also fills a gap in scholarship on non-Judeo-Christian philanthropic traditions and makes important strides toward an understanding of the historic relationship between the government and the voluntary sector prefacing the growth of the welfare state.

As a graduate student, I have combined research and teaching. At Harvard, I have designed and led a year-long tutorial (seminar) on modern Chinese history for honors-track undergraduates and taught two sections of an introductory course on the social anthropology of China. In these courses, organized as discussion seminars, I stress a range of skills: writing, critical reading, and persuasive oral presentation; I also challenge students to consider changing gender roles in Chinese society. Students have been generous in expressing their appreciation of my enthusiasm for the material and my dedication to improving their writing and analytical abilities; I would be glad to send their letters and course evaluations to you at your convenience.

My interdepartmental teaching experience and my training in pre-modern Chinese history, modern Chinese history, and social anthropology have made me a devout believer in interdisciplinary study. I am excited to see Williams' extensive course offerings in anthropology, political science, and Asian American history, all fruitful areas for cross-disciplinary cooperation, complementing and adding complexity to the teaching of history. I am particularly interested in working with Williams' Asian Studies and Women's Studies programs to build on these interdisciplinary opportunities.

At Harvard, I have taken an active role in fostering academic community. Skills I developed while working in academic administration in Washington have enabled me to build bridges within and between disciplines through activities such as organizing an interdisciplinary lunch series at Harvard's Center for International Affairs (long a bastion of Political Science); founding and editing a graduate student journal; assisting in ongoing joint curriculum development of the East Asian Studies program; and serving as a non-academic advisor to Harvard undergraduates. My experience teaching and advising students, my administrative abilities, my familiarity with living and studying abroad and with the process of placing students in overseas programs, as well as my commitment to the larger ideals of a liberal arts education all combine to make me and Williams an ideal match.

I am enclosing my curriculum vitae and course descriptions; my dossier (including letters from Professors Philip Kuhn, William Kirby, James Watson, and Ezra Vogel) will be forwarded to you separately. Please let me know if I can provide additional information or writing samples to aid you in the evaluation of my application. I look forward to hearing from you.

Sincerely,

Catherine Ryan

Commentary: Catherine Ryan's letter (1 1/2 pages on normal paper) demonstrates tailoring to the teaching and community service needs of a small liberal arts college, particularly to the teaching needs of Williams, which she has researched. Her dissertation discussion is longer than usual, probably because she has not appended a summary. It effectively brings out the significance of her thesis, although she neglects to mention her future research. The c.v. places her impressive "Fellowships and Awards" at the beginning and her "Conference Papers and Publications" ahead of "Teaching Experience" (it could go either way for a teaching college). She got the Williams job.

CATHERINE RYAN

History and East Asian Languages
Harvard University
Cambridge, MA 02138

000 K Street, #40
Boston, MA 02000
(617) 001-2345
e-mail: ryan@fas.harvard.edu

EDUCATION

HARVARD UNIVERSITY
PhD, November 1996. History and East Asian Languages (late Qing/Republican China).
General Examination Fields: Pre-modern China, Modern China, Social Anthropology.

UNIVERSITY OF PARIS III (Oriental Languages and Civilizations)
Diplôme Supérieur, 1985. Field: Contemporary Chinese Studies. Emphasis on PRC
international and regional relations.

HARVARD UNIVERSITY
AB, *magna cum laude*, 1984. Concentration: East Asian Languages and Civilizations
(China). Semester abroad at Peking University (CIEE Chinese Language Program).

DISSERTATION

"The Power of Mercy: The Early History of the Chinese Red Cross Society, 1900-1937."
Advisor: Professor Philip Kuhn.

FELLOWSHIPS AND AWARDS

Albert Gallatin Fellowship in International Affairs	1995
Harvard University Graduate Society Dissertation Fellowship Alternate	1995
Harvard University Center for International Affairs Summer Research Grant	1995
Foreign Language and Area Studies (FLAS) Grant for dissertation research	1994
Committee on Scholarly Communication with China Research Grant Extension	1994
CSCC Research Grant for twelve months of dissertation research in Nanjing, PRC	1993
Harvard University Sheldon Travel Grant for dissertation research	1993
Academic-year FLAS for preliminary dissertation research	1992
NCR Foundation Research Grant for research in Taipei, ROC	1992
Harvard Club of the Republic of China Research Grant for research in Taipei, ROC	1992
Summer FLAS for third-year intensive Japanese, Harvard University	1991
Tower Fellowship for study in France	1984

CONFERENCE PAPERS AND PUBLICATIONS

"Social Action and Elite Identity: The Chinese Red Cross Society in Late Qing and
Republican China," in Papers on Chinese History (1996), forthcoming.

"Co-opting the State: Philanthropy and Local Government in Republican China."
Delivered at Annual Meeting of the Association of Asian Studies, Honolulu, HI, April
13, 1996.

"The Changing Nature of Philanthropy in Late Qing and Republican China." Delivered
at Annual Meeting of the Association for Asian Studies, Washington, DC, April 7, 1995.

"The Introduction of International Humanitarian Norms into China: The Case of the
Chinese Red Cross Society." Delivered at the Center for International Affairs, Harvard
University, March 22, 1995, and the Fourth Annual Graduate Student Conference on
Asia, Columbia University, February 12, 1995.

TEACHING EXPERIENCE

HARVARD UNIVERSITY, Core Program & Anthropology Department
Teaching Fellow, *Anthropology of China* (Professor James Watson): Spring 1993.
Taught two sections of introductory anthropology of China.

HARVARD UNIVERSITY, East Asian Studies Department
Tutor, *Junior Tutorial, China*: Fall 1990; Fall, Spring 1991-1992. Taught own syllabus
on late imperial through contemporary China to third-year EAS honors concentrators in
discussion seminar format.

CLARK UNIVERSITY, Nathan Mayhew Seminars (Summer School)
Instructor: Summer 1990. Designed and taught course for summer students on the
Tiananmen Square incident in historical perspective.

RELATED PROFESSIONAL EXPERIENCE

HARVARD UNIVERSITY, East Asian Studies Department
Assistant Head Tutor: Fall, Spring 1994-1996. Administrative director and academic
advisor for undergraduate East Asian Studies program. Oversaw seven teachers and fifty
third-year students. Responsible for publication of *East Asian Studies Newsletter*.

HARVARD UNIVERSITY, Winthrop House
Non-Resident Tutor: Fall 1990-Present. Academic and non-academic advising;
organized and ran weekly Chinese language table; served on House grant selection
committee (Rockefeller and Truman grants).

PAPERS ON CHINESE HISTORY
Editor, graduate student journal: 1992, 1993, 1995 editions. Worked with 4-member
student board to found journal, edit and prepare publication of student papers on issues in
Song, Ming, Qing and Republican history.

HARVARD UNIVERSITY, Graduate Student Council
History and East Asian Languages Representative: Fall 1990-Fall 1992. Represented
Department at monthly meetings; served on Spring 1992 GSC travel grant selection
committee. International Student Host, 1990-1992.

COMMITTEE ON SCHOLARLY COMMUNICATION WITH CHINA
Program Assistant, National Program for Advanced Study and Research in China: 1987-
1988. Administered grants for study in China to American students and scholars.

RESEARCH AFFILIATIONS

Graduate Student Associate, Harvard Center for International Affairs   1994-1995
Visiting Scholar, Nanjing University, Nanjing, PRC. Research conducted at Number
Two Historical Archives, Nanjing; Municipal Archives, Shanghai; Number One
Historical Archives, Beijing; Municipal Archives, Beijing; Archival Section of the
Chinese Red Cross Society, Beijing   1993-1994
Visiting Scholar, Archives of the Federation of Red Cross and Red Crescent Societies,
Geneva, Switzerland   1993, 1995
Visiting Scholar, Academia Sinica, Taipei, ROC   1992

LANGUAGES

Mandarin Chinese: excellent. Classical Chinese: reading. French: excellent. Japanese:
reading.

December 6, 1993

George Thornton
000 Main St., Apt. 3
Cambridge, MA 02139
tel. (617) 497-0000

Professor Susan Cianci, Chair
Nineteenth Century Search Committee
Department of History of Art
University of Pennsylvania
Philadelphia, PA 19104

Dear Professor Cianci:

I am most eager to apply for the position of assistant professor posted in the
November edition of the CAA *Job Listings*. I will obtain my Ph.D. in art history
from Harvard University this coming June; my field of study is Western art from the
18th century to the present, with a specialization in 19th-century European art.
Because of my commitment to both detailed historical analysis and continual re-
evaluation of contemporary theory in my work and teaching, I believe I am a strong
candidate for this position.

My dissertation focuses on the paintings of Théodore Rousseau (1812-1867), the
leader of the Barbizon School, whose controversial landscapes have never been
examined in depth. Revising the traditional study of a single artist in light of recent
debates in critical theory concerning authorship, I develop three ways of interpreting
Rousseau's landscapes, based on extensive primary research concerning the singular
formal structures of the paintings, Rousseau's writings and lifestyle, and the cultural
significance of several important sites he painted. In so doing, I find semiology to be
an insufficient model for interpreting landscape, and I specifically elaborate a theory
of how Rousseau's works may be seen to instill ecological consciousness in the
viewer.

Other domains of art history in which I have particular expertise are the general
history and theory of landscape, the history of prints in the 19th century, the work of
Courbet, and romanticism.

I have had teaching experience of several kinds, as indicated on my c.v. In addition
to conducting discussion sections for courses in both 19th- and 20th-century art, I
have taught my own undergraduate seminar on landscape, which compared a
number of artists from Dürer to Cézanne and Guo Xi to Frank Lloyd Wright. This
January I will be teaching my own lecture course at Tufts University on European
art from the 1780s through the 1850s. To fill the needs of the job in your
department, I feel prepared immediately to teach 19th-century art and participate in
surveys, and to teach 500- and 700-level courses on topics such as romantic
landscape theory and practice, Courbet, and French landscape in relation to travel,
urbanism, and industrialization. In addition, I would be happy to participate in the
university's writing requirement, having had special training in undergraduate
writing enhancement that included teaching writing-intensive discussion sections.

Besides the high quality of the University of Pennsylvania generally and the art history faculty in particular, the excellent museum resources of Philadelphia for both teaching purposes and my own research make the job especially attractive to me. Enclosed are my curriculum vitae, which includes a dissertation summary and the names of three references, and a copy of the exhibition essay I wrote three years ago. I will attend the CAA conference in New York this February, where I will also present a paper entitled "Co-Constructing Biography: Alfred Sensier, Théodore Rousseau, and Jean-François Millet" in an Open Session on February 19.

Thank you for considering my application.

Sincerely,

George Thornton

Commentary: This straightforward letter is tailored to the institution, especially in the "Teaching Experience" section. Given that he is applying for a position in a research university, George Thornton might have briefly discussed his future research projects in the letter and considered a "Work in Progress" section for the vita. He also might have elaborated slightly on the other domains of expertise mentioned in paragraph three, especially if they were relevant for the job. In the c.v., the section on "Museum Experience" is typical but rather terse; he probably would have included more explanation if it were relevant for the job. Although he did not get this job, Thornton did receive campus interviews and an offer from a Midwestern research university.

GEORGE THORNTON

Department of Fine Arts
Sackler Museum
Harvard University
Cambridge, MA 02138

000 Main St., Apt. 3
Cambridge, MA 02139
tel. (617) 497-0000

EDUCATION:

Ph.D., Art History	Harvard University	June 1994 (expected)
M.A., Art History	Harvard University	November 1989
Special student, Art History	Institute of European Studies and the University of Paris IV	January-June, 1986
Special student, Art History	University of Pittsburgh	January-December, 1985
B.A., Physics	Washington University (St. Louis)	May 1984

ACADEMIC HONORS AND GRANTS:

Charlotte W. Newcombe Doctoral Dissertation Fellowship, 1992-93
Harvard Lurcy Traveling Fellowship, 1991-92
UCLA Art Council Summer Fellowship, Summer 1990
Susan and Richard Smith Foundation Fellowship, 1988-89
German Academic Exchange Service grant, summer language study in
Augsburg, Germany, Summer 1988
National Merit Scholarship recipient, 1980-84

DISSERTATION:

"Théodore Rousseau and the Ecological Landscape," Professor Henri Zerner,
adviser (see attached dissertation summary)

PUBLICATION AND PAPER PRESENTATION:

"The Re-Design of Nature: Graphic Constructions of Natural Space in Europe,
1760-1860," essay and exhibition at the Grunwald Center for the Graphic Arts,
University of California in Los Angeles, April-May, 1991

"Co-constructing Biography: Alfred Sensier, Théodore Rousseau, and Jean-
François Millet," paper to be delivered at the College Art Association Annual
Conference, New York, February 1994

TEACHING EXPERIENCE: (all at Harvard University except the first course)

Visiting Lecturer, "Romanticism and Realism," Tufts University, Spring 1994:
Will teach a lecture course of my design to about twenty-five
undergraduate and graduate students; the course examines individual artists
in France, England, Germany, and Spain, emphasizing issues related to
prints and mass media, the social role of the artist, structures of exhibition
and patronage, and the centrality of landscape to modernism.

Head Teaching Fellow, "Romanticism," Professor Henri Zerner, Fall 1990: Responsible for the administration of the course (arranging discussion sections, organizing paper assignments and exams, helping mount an exhibition) and teaching one weekly discussion section; the course studied romantic art throughout Europe and its relation to literature, music, and philosophy.
Teaching Fellow for same course, Fall 1988.

Junior Tutorial Instructor, "Landscape Painters and the Land," Spring 1990: Designed and taught a seminar course for seven juniors majoring in art history; the course was a comparative study of landscape artists from the 16th to the 20th centuries, in Europe, in the United States, and in China; students wrote in-depth papers on a range of topics related to landscape.

Teaching Fellow, "Early Modern Painting," Professor Jean-Claude Lebensztejn, Fall 1989: Designed and led two weekly discussion sections, and graded papers and exams; the course treated European art from the 1880s through the 1930s.

Teaching Fellow, "Modern Art and Abstraction," Professor Anna Chave, Spring 1989: Led two weekly discussion sections, and graded papers and exams; the course covered material from the 1890s through the 1960s.

Graduate Writing Fellow, Spring 1989: Participated in a training program that introduces graduate teaching fellows to methods of improving undergraduate writing skills.

MUSEUM EXPERIENCE:

Research Fellow, the Grunwald Center for the Graphic Arts, University of California at Los Angeles, Summer 1990

Curatorial Assistant, Department of Prints, Fogg Art Museum, Harvard University, Cambridge, MA, June 1989-May 1990

AREAS OF TEACHING COMPETENCE:

Art in Europe and America, 18th-20th centuries; 19th-century French painting; 19th-century prints; Romanticism; theory and general history of landscape; art history and semiotics

FOREIGN LANGUAGES:

French: fluent reading, excellent speaking
German: good reading and speaking
Chinese: beginning level, Mandarin

EXTENDED FOREIGN TRAVEL:

Dissertation research in France, September 1991-August 1992
Language study in Augsburg, Germany, June-July 1988
Study in Paris, France, January-June 1986

ACADEMIC REFERENCES: Department of Fine Arts, Sackler Museum, Harvard University, Cambridge, MA 02138, office tel. (617) 495-0000
[Three references appended in the original are not included here.]

DISSERTATION SUMMARY

Théodore Rousseau (1812-1867) was considered in his lifetime the leading
landscape painter of the avant-garde and as great a painter as Corot. Nevertheless,
Alfred Sensier's detailed biography of his friend, published in 1872, remains the
only major study of Rousseau's work, and only now is a *catalogue raisonné* being
undertaken in France. The present dissertation analyzes Rousseau's paintings in
depth for the first time, attempts to restructure the monograph as a genre in light of
postmodern critiques of authorship, and develops three different approaches to the
interpretation of landscapes. A major claim is that Rousseau gave his paintings
ecological meaning, at a time when the concept of ecology was at its inception.

The first chapter traces the history of Rousseau's reputation. It demonstrates
that his early renown as a political radical was exaggerated, and also argues that our
continuing view of the Barbizon School painters as precursors to Impressionism is a
misconception.

Chapter two opens the first approach to analyzing meaning in the pictures.
Describing specific visual devices invented by Rousseau, it shows how his paintings
drain narrativity from the landscape and enact a tension in the actual experience of
viewing between belonging to and displacement from the landscape. Semiotics is
found to be insufficient as an explanation of how meaning thus occurs; the idea of
"sensational meaning" is developed as an alternative, laying the groundwork for
defining an ecological landscape manner.

Chapter three considers biographical meanings from Rousseau's extensive (and
mostly unpublished) correspondence and from his life. Arguing that his statements
must be considered not as intentions but as statements aimed at directing critical
interpretation, it reveals Rousseau devaluing narrativity as a source of meaning in
his art, redefining composition and modeling, and advocating a kind of ecological
identification with trees. It also examines how he shaped his actual life as an
interpretative framework for the paintings, both in his daily habits and in his
relationships with friends and patrons.

"Site ideology" is the subject of chapter four. By comparing Rousseau's
depiction of several key sites to other representations of those sites in guidebooks,
geographies, literature, and art, the chapter shows Rousseau undermining
picturesque aesthetics to inflect the ideology surrounding rural France. His way of
depicting wasteland in Berry and Landes, for example, carefully avoids
romanticizing rural life, making the viewer empathize with highly austere terrain
that was considered to have no aesthetic value.

The final chapter considers the romantic roots, the politics, and the aesthetics
of ecology in the 19th century. It unveils Rousseau's concrete activities as a
conservationist while living at Barbizon, next to the forest of Fontainebleau; it
develops the notion of ecological meaning in pictures; and it suggests how we might
connect ecology and painting as kindred forms of representation.

Documentary research for the dissertation, conducted during a yearlong visit to
France in 1991-92, included extensive work with Rousseau's letters at the Louvre
and elsewhere; the uncovering of specific regulations concerning French

forests and land usage at the National Archives, provincial archives, and the French National Office of Forests; travel to Rousseau's most important sites; investigation of regional geographical literature; and examination of papers and manuscripts of Alfred Sensier. In addition to initiating discussion of Rousseau's important and unusual work, the dissertation should add to the growing literature on landscape theory, contribute to current debates concerning semiotics and visual art, and open up discussion of how ecology may have informed art, and vice versa, in the 19th century.

Jeffrey Liebman

National Bureau of Economic Research
1050 Massachusetts Avenue
Cambridge, MA 02138
(617) 868-3900 x000

300 Walker Street, Apt. 2
Jamaica Plain, MA 02130
(617) 983-0000
liebman@harvard.edu

EDUCATION

Harvard University, Cambridge, MA
   Ph.D., Economics (expected June 1996).

Yale University, New Haven, CT
   B.A., *magna cum laude*, May 1989.
   Distinction in Economics and Political Science.
   Ronald Meltzer Economics Award for outstanding senior essay in
      major.

HONORS AND AWARDS

Alfred P. Sloan Foundation Doctoral Dissertation Fellowship, 1995-1996.

National Science Foundation Graduate Research Fellowship, 1991-1994.

Certificate of Distinction in Teaching, Harvard University, 1994.

Tinker Foundation Fellowship for research in Mexico, Summer 1992.

FIELDS OF INTEREST

Public Economics, Labor Economics, Applied Econometrics.

DISSERTATION TITLE

The Impact of the Earned Income Tax Credit on Labor Supply and Taxpayer
   Compliance (see attached abstract).

COMPLETED PAPERS

"Labor Supply Response to the Earned Income Tax Credit" (with Nada
   Eissa), NBER Working Paper 5158, June 1995, forthcoming in the
   Quarterly Journal of Economics.

"Noncompliance and the Earned Income Tax Credit: Taxpayer Error or
   Taxpayer Fraud?" October 1995.

"Who Are the Ineligible Earned Income Tax Credit Recipients?" September
   1995.

RESEARCH IN PROGRESS

"A Dynamic Structural Model of Female Labor Supply and Welfare Participation with an Application to the Optimal Phase-out of the Earned Income Tax Credit."

"An Evaluation of HUD's Moving to Opportunity Program" (with Lawrence Katz and Jeffrey Kling).

"Taxes and the Composition of CEO Compensation" (with Brian Hall).

TEACHING EXPERIENCE

Section Leader, *Principles of Economics*, Fall 1993-Spring 1994.

Teaching Fellow, *American Economic Policy*, Spring 1995.

Teaching Fellow, *Research in Public Finance*, Fall 1994-Spring 1995.

REFERENCES

Professor Martin Feldstein, Department of Economics, Harvard University.

Professor Lawrence Katz, Department of Economics, Harvard University.

Professor David Cutler, Department of Economics, Harvard University.

Professor Guido Imbens, Department of Economics, Harvard University.

Commentary: Jeffrey Liebman's c.v. was fashioned for research universities; hence, he underplays his teaching experience and omits three years of work experience between college and graduate school (unusual, since it was economics related, but he wanted to emphasize his current research). Also unusual for economists is that all of the chapters of his thesis were on a single topic; in the original vita, the abstract was unconventionally placed on the first page just below "Fields of Interest," highlighting his strengths. Liebman had several fly-outs and a number of offers from top-rated departments.

DISSERTATION ABSTRACT
The Impact of the Earned Income Tax Credit on Labor Supply and Taxpayer
Compliance

After major expansions in the tax reform acts of 1986, 1990, and 1993,
the earned income tax credit (EITC) has emerged as a central part of the
federal government's efforts to reduce poverty and welfare dependency
among families with children. The EITC differs in two important ways from
other programs designed to assist needy families with children. First, the
EITC creates different labor supply incentives than do programs such as
AFDC and food stamps. Second, the EITC is administered through the tax
system rather than through the welfare system. The four chapters of my
dissertation examine these two features of the EITC.

The first chapter examines the impact of the Tax Reform Act of 1987,
which included an expansion of the EITC, on the labor force participation
and hours of work of single women with children. It concludes that, between
1984-1986 and 1988-1990, single women with children increased their
relative labor force participation by up to 2.8 percentage points. Over this
time period there was no decline in the relative hours of work of single
women with children who were already in the labor force. The second
chapter estimates a dynamic structural model of labor supply and welfare
participation in order to examine the optimal phase-out of the earned
income tax credit. The basic monthly model is a 5-choice multinomial probit
which is estimated using a Bayesian technique, the Gibbs sampler. Annual
tax incentives are incorporated into the model by specifying the choice
problem as maximizing the sum of utility in the current month and expected
utility for the rest of the year. Dynamic programming is used to solve this
choice problem.

The third chapter uses an exact match of the March 1991 CPS to
information from the tax returns of CPS adults in order to determine how
many ineligible taxpayers receive the EITC. The performance of three
multiple imputation methods is compared in accounting for sample members
who could not be matched to tax returns. I find that 13 percent of EITC
recipients did not have a child in their CPS household when they received
the credit. This is likely to be a lower bound for EITC noncompliance.

The fourth chapter examines whether EITC noncompliance is taxpayer
error or taxpayer fraud. Using the 1985 and 1988 IRS Taxpayer
Compliance Measurement Surveys, I test whether the probability that a
childless taxpayer claims a child on his or her tax return depends on the
amount of the EITC available to the taxpayer. If noncompliance responds to
the returns to such behavior, then it is unlikely to be due to inadvertent
error. I estimate that at least one-third of ineligible EITC recipients evade
taxes (and obtain refunds) due to the incentive for evasion created by the
EITC.

ALBERT PIÑON

00 Willow Avenue
Medford, MA 02155
Tel. (617) 396-6000
e-mail: apinon@fas.harvard.edu

Department of Political Science
New School for Social Research
New York, NY 10003
Tel. (212) 229-0000
Fax. (212) 807-0000

EDUCATION

HARVARD UNIVERSITY, Ph.D. in Government, June 1991.

SUSSEX UNIVERSITY, B.A. (First Class Honors) in Politics, 1982.

UNIVERSITY OF CALIFORNIA, SAN DIEGO, various courses, 1977-79.

AREAS OF SPECIALIZATION

Prepared to Teach: Democratic Transitions and Consolidation in Latin America, State Forms in the Third World, Latin American Politics.

Research Interests: Military Regimes in Latin America, Democratic Transitions, Judicial Reform in Latin America.

EXPERIENCE

Teaching

Assistant Professor, New School for Social Research, Department of Political Science, 1991-present. (On leave, 1996-97.)

Visiting Assistant Professor, Harvard University Government Department, Spring 1995.

Teaching Fellow, Harvard University Government Department, 1986-91. Taught sections for American Politics (1989), Comparative Politics (1986, 1990, and 1991), The Cuban Revolution (1989/90), and Modern India (1987).

Instructor, Upward Bound, Sacramento, CA, Summers 1980-85.
Taught political science and Californian politics and counseled students for a Federal program for low-income high school students.

Research

Associate, Rockefeller Center for Latin American and Iberian Studies, Harvard University, 1996-97.

Research Fellow, Program on Nonviolent Sanctions, Center for International Affairs, Harvard University, Spring 1995.

Research Fellow, Fulbright Scholar Program, São Paulo, Brazil, 1994.

Associate, Harvard's Center for International Affairs, 1989-91.

Research (continued)

Doctoral Fellow, Center for Business and Government, John F. Kennedy School of Government, Summer 1989.

Doctoral Fellow, Federal University of Pernambuco, Recife, Brazil, 1987-88.

University Service

Member, Library Committee, New School for Social Research, 1992-95.

Member, Committee on Historical Studies, Committee on the Study of Democracy, and Core Faculty of the Janey Program in Latin American Studies, New School for Social Research, 1991-present.

Other

Consultant, "Linha Directa, Linha Aberta" (Program for Angola), Voice of America, 1996.

Consultant, United Nations Development Programme, 1994 and 1997.

International Polling Station Officer, United Nations, Cambodia, May-June 1993.

International Election Observer, International Foundation for Electoral Systems, Angola, September-October 1992.

Legislative Researcher, Legi-Tech Corporation, Sacramento, California, 1984.

Fellow, State Senate, Sacramento, California, Summer 1979.

AWARDS

Einstein Institution Fellowship, Spring Semester 1995.
Fulbright Senior Scholar award for research in Brazil, 1994.
Edward M. Chase Dissertation Prize, Harvard University, 1991.
Harvard University Certificate of Distinction in Teaching, 1991.
Tinker Foundation Summer Research Grants, 1985 and 1990.
Inter-American Foundation Research Fellowship, 1987-89.
Organization of American States Research Fellowship, 1987-88.
Harvard University Core Program Teaching Certificate, 1987.

LANGUAGES

Fluent in Portuguese and working knowledge of Spanish and French.

PROFESSIONAL AFFILIATIONS

Member, American Political Science Association.
Member, Brazil Seminar, Columbia University.
Member, Latin American Studies Association.

PUBLICATIONS

Book Manuscript

The End of the Peasantry: The Emergence of the Rural Labor Movement in Northeast Brazil (University of Pittsburgh Press, forthcoming, Spring 1997).

Book Chapters

"The Crisis of Developmentalism and the Rural Labor Movement in Northeast Brazil," in Douglas Chalmers, Carlos Vilas, Katherine Roberts-Hite et al. (eds.), The New Politics of Inequality in Latin America: Rethinking Participation and Representation (New York: Oxford University Press, forthcoming, March 1997).

"The Effects of Agricultural Modernization," in Unner Kirdar and Leonard Silk (eds.), Global Change: Social Conflict or Harmony? (New York: New York University Press/UNDP, 1995).

Refereed Journal Articles

"'Persecution and Farce': The Origins and Transformation of Brazil's Political Trials" in Latin American Research Review, forthcoming, Vol. 33, No. 1, Spring 1998.

"Making Democracy for Workers: The Brazilian Working Class and Labor Movement in Comparative Perspective" in International Labor and Working-Class History, Spring 1996.

"The Neglected Tragedy: The Return to War in Angola, 1992-93" in the Journal of Modern African Studies, Vol. 32, No. 1, March 1994.

"Economic Development, Democracy, and Civil Society in the Third World: the Northeastern Brazilian Case" in Third World Quarterly, Vol. 14, No. 2, November 1993.

"Agrarian Reform and the Rural Workers' Unions of the Pernambuco Sugar Zone, Brazil 1985-1988" in Journal of Developing Areas, January 1992.

"Profeta no Exílio: O Retorno do Mito de Francisco Julião" in Cadernos de Estudos Sociais (Recife, Brazil), Vol. 17, No. 1, January/June 1991.

Other Scholarly Journal Articles

"Latin America in the Era of 'Hot Money'" in Dissent, Winter 1996.

Co-editor and author of introduction to an issue of Latin American Perspectives entitled "Labor and the Free Market in the Americas," Issue 84, Vol. 22, No. 1, Winter 1995.

[Five additional articles written between 1989 and 1994 are omitted here.]

Working Papers

"The Shackled Monster: State Violence and Legal Repression in Brazil, 1964 to the Present," synopsis of presentation to the seminar of the Program on Nonviolent Sanctions and Cultural Survival, Center for International Affairs, Harvard University, August 1995.

"Democratic Change?" Center for Studies of Social Change Working Paper No. 193, New School for Social Research, August 1994.

"Rural Labor and the End of Military Rule in Northeast Brazil," Working Paper No. 6, Janey Program on Latin America, New School for Social Research, April 1993.

EDITORIAL WORK

Reviewer for <u>Comparative Politics</u>, <u>Latin American Perspectives</u>, and <u>Political Power and Social Theory</u>.

JOURNALISM

"Más Allá de los Pronósticos" (article on Cuba) in <u>Observador Internacional</u> (Mexico City), Ano 1, Número 2, July 25, 1993.

"Waffling on Angolan Future Hardly Serves U.S. Interests" in the <u>Sacramento Bee</u>, January 6, 1993.

[Twelve other articles written between 1982 and 1992 are omitted.]

REFERENCES

[Two references are omitted here.]

Commentary: This vita is included to represent a "softer" social scientist with a few years of academic experience. Note that, while Albert Piñon (correctly) condenses his teaching fellow experience, he chooses to leave in his Upward Bound teaching (probably to give a fuller picture of who he is). A separate "Courses Taught" section would be helpful in this c.v. Because the "Publications" list is now extensive, it is customarily placed at the end and subdivided into categories. In the interest of space, several publications have been omitted. For most universities, it would have been more prudent to condense or summarize the list of journalistic publications anyway.

ANLIAN WU

Department of East Asian Languages and Civilizations
Harvard University
2 Divinity Avenue
Cambridge, MA 02138
(617) 495-0000

29 Eliot St., Apt. 4
Cambridge, MA 02139
(617) 491-0000

EDUCATION

Harvard University	Ph.D., joint degree in East Asian Languages and Civilizations/Social Anthropology	June 1995 (expected)
Harvard University	M.A., East Asian Languages and Civilizations	June 1990
Chinese Academy of Social Sciences	M.A., Social Anthropology	May 1986
Higher Education Examination Committee, PRC	B.A., English	September 1983

DISSERTATION

"Cosmology and the Transformation of Political Culture in Early China," Harvard University, 1995 (See attached dissertation summary.)

PUBLICATIONS

"*Wuxing* and the Formation of the Han Empire," in *Yin Yang Wuxing Tanyuan (The Origins and Development of Five Element Theory)*, ed. Sarah Allan, Jiangsu Guji Press (forthcoming, 1995)

"Disciplining the Body at the Pivot of the Universe: The Construction of China's Emperorship," *Festschrift* in honor of K. C. Chang, eds. Robert E. Murowchick, Lothar von Falkenhausen, Cheng-hwa Tsang, and Robin D. S. Yates, Taipei and Cambridge, Academia Sinica and the Peabody Museum of Harvard University (forthcoming, 1996)

"Wa," *Encyclopedia of World Cultures*, New Haven: Human Relations Area Files, 1990

"On Ethnological Studies," in *Minzhuxue Yanju (The Studies of Nationalities)*, vol. 7, 1983 (in Chinese)

PAPERS AND PRESENTATIONS

"From *Sifang* to *Wuxing*: Cosmology and Power in Transition," an article submitted to *Comparative Studies in Society and History*

"Culture, State, and Person in the Making of Emperorship," a panel organized for Association of Asian Studies Annual Meeting, Washington, D.C., April 1995

"Cosmology, Emperorship, and the Han Empire," to be presented at the Association of Asian Studies Annual Meeting, Washington, D.C., April 1995

PAPERS AND PRESENTATIONS (continued)

"Wuxing Cosmology and the Transformation of Political Culture in Early China," the Association of Asian Studies Annual Meeting, Boston, March 1994

"Distinction and Integration: Eastern Zhou's Heritage of Huang Lao Daoism," New England Conference of the Association of Asian Studies, Smith College, October 1990

"The Idea of *Tian* (Heaven) in *Zuozhuan,*" The Graduate Student Conference on Chinese Studies, Harvard University, May 1990

ACADEMIC HONORS AND GRANTS

Dissertation Fellowship, Harvard Yen-ching Institute, 1993-94
Doctoral Scholarship for Junior Faculty, Harvard Yen-ching Institute, 1986-90
Middlebury College Scholarship for Summer School, Summer 1989

TEACHING EXPERIENCE (at Harvard University)

Senior Thesis Adviser, East Asian Studies, Fall 1994-Spring 1995: Provided academic guidance for seniors writing their theses.

Assistant Head Tutor for Sophomores, East Asian Studies, Fall 1992-Spring 1993: Served as the academic adviser for all sophomore concentrators in East Asian Studies, advising on decisions such as course selection, study abroad projects, and departmental requirements.

Junior Tutor, East Asian Studies, Spring 1991: Advised junior concentrators in East Asian Languages and Civilizations on independent research projects and the writing of research papers.

Tutorial Instructor
   "The History of Modern China," Junior Tutorial, East Asian Studies, Fall 1990: Designed and taught a seminar course for all East Asian Studies juniors with a concentration in China. This interdisciplinary course covered the history of China from the late imperial period to the contemporary era, drawing theories, methodology, and material from history, anthropology, sociology, literature, and gender studies. It was aimed at fostering both analytical and research abilities.

   "The History of Pre-Modern China," Sophomore Tutorial, East Asian Studies, Fall 1989 and Spring 1990: Designed and taught a seminar course for all sophomores with a concentration in East Asian Studies–China. The course covered the history of China from the Bronze Age (2000 B.C.) to the end of the imperial period (1911).

Graduate Writing Fellow, 1989: Participated in a training program that introduces graduate teaching fellows to methods of improving undergraduate writing skills.

Teaching Fellow
   "Tradition and Transformation in East Asian Civilization: China," Professors Wei Ming Tu and Peter Bol, Fall 1989: Led weekly discussions, commented on papers, and graded examinations.

TEACHING EXPERIENCE (continued)

Teaching Fellow
"Ancient Chinese Art and Religion," Professor Wu Hung, Fall 1988: Led weekly discussions and guided analysis of art objects in museums.

"Advanced Conversational Chinese," Fall 1989-Spring 1990, and Fall 1994

SPECIALIZATION

Teaching:
History of China and East Asia, premodern and modern periods
Social anthropology and critical theory
Philosophy and religion of China
Art and Archaeology of East Asia
Comparative studies of ancient civilizations
Gender studies of East Asia

Research:
Political discourse and imperial institutions
The construction of cultural unity in China
Comparative studies of cosmology, kingship, and empires
Nationalism and identity in modern China
Gender in premodern and modern China

FIELD EXPERIENCE

Two ethnic groups—Wa and Jimo—living in the mountains of Yunnan Province, Southwest China, Fall 1985-Spring 1986; conducted as research for a master's thesis on the transitions in the culture, economic life, and environment of these ethnic minorities under the interventions of the Communist central government.

FOREIGN LANGUAGES

Chinese: native speaker, excellent reading of classical Chinese
Japanese: very good reading and elementary speaking
French: good reading and speaking

ACADEMIC REFERENCES

[Three references listed in the original are omitted here.]

COSMOLOGY AND THE TRANSFORMATION OF
POLITICAL CULTURE IN EARLY CHINA

Dissertation Summary, Anlian Wu, Harvard University

This dissertation investigates how cosmology, a cornerstone of "Chinese culture" that still informs everyday life today, was fabricated in its early historical context during the transition from the Bronze Age to the imperial era in the last four centuries B.C. It is the first work to trace the changing links between political power and cosmology from the Bronze Age to the early empires. It also contends that cosmology was a political discourse used by rival social forces for political contestation, rather than a homogeneous belief system. Finally, it argues that the essential imperial institution—emperorship—was built into the core of cosmology. The goal of the dissertation is to disclose the social conflicts that were veiled by a seemingly coherent cosmology, and thus to test and enrich theories about cosmology, kingship, and political power with the case of ancient China.

Appraising the scholarly commentary on cosmology from the perspectives of both history and anthropology, the first of six chapters challenges the traditional view of cosmology as a homogeneous entity distinct from society, either a mystification of the political order or a pre-existing structure of ideas which social reality imitates. It urges the return of cosmology to the political process that produced it and manifested the conflicts embodied in it, and suggests three approaches to doing so.

Based on material cultural remains, oracle bone and bronze inscriptions, and texts recently unearthed as well as transmitted, chapters two and three develop the first approach—analyzing historical changes in the conjunction between cosmology and power. In the Bronze Age, the ruling clan conceived of the universe in terms of four quarters surrounding the center, the center being the king's body and his ancestral line, through which the world of the gods and the world of human beings communicated. This centrality was the key to the political domination and divine authority of the kings. Yet in the Warring States period, when political domination by a royal clan gave way to competition among hegemons, *Wuxing* cosmology emerged to replace the notion of a sacred and eternal center with dynamic interactions of five cosmic phases, substituting direct correlations of the human world and the cosmos for the medium of the royal ancestors.

Chapter four develops a second approach to cosmology, exploring the discursive function of *Wuxing* in the formation of the early empires. Focusing on the synthetic representation of *Wuxing* discourse—"Wuxing Zhi" in *Hanshu*—it shows how conflicting political forces used this cosmology in debating imperial sovereignty and the transmission of power, in contesting their political goals, and in competing for moral authority.

The construction of emperorship, the subject of chapter five, is the basis for the third approach. Examining theories of omen and resonance in *Wuxing* cosmology, this chapter demonstrates how these theories constructed emperorship as the responsible agent for the cosmic-social order, the pivot of power relations, and the exemplary body for subject formations.

The concluding chapter synthesizes these three approaches and discusses their historical, comparative, and theoretical implications, unveiling the impact of the cosmological constructions of emperorship and imperial sovereignty on actual emperors and politics, drawing comparisons from cosmologies and kingship from other civilizations, and suggesting how cultural-historical heritages such as cosmology and empire have been revived in modern power contests in China.

Commentary: This c.v. is clearly tailored for a research university, leading with "Publications," followed by "Papers and Presentations," and even putting the extensive "Teaching Experience" after "Academic Honors and Grants." The "Field Experience" section is obligatory for anthropologists, but is generally put toward the end—especially in this case, since Anlian Wu is presenting herself as a historian of early China. Wu accepted an offer from a Midwestern research university.

HARVARD UNIVERSITY

LYMAN LABORATORY OF PHYSICS
CAMBRIDGE, MA 02138
TELEX: 9102008000 (HARV BSN)
CARTER@PHYSICS.HARVARD.EDU

ETHAN D. CARTER
TEL: 617-495-1000
FAX: 617-496-8000

January 12, 1995

Professor Arnold Case
Department of Physics
Wake Forest University
Winston-Salem, NC 27109

Dear Professor Case:

I am writing to apply for a faculty position in the Physics Department at Wake Forest University. I am currently an Associate Professor of Physics at Harvard University specializing in particle astrophysics and particle phenomenology. I have enclosed all of the requested application materials.

My current research and planned future research emphasize particle astrophysics, and this seems to fit very well with your job description. I have taught both physics and astrophysics courses at the undergraduate and graduate level, and I have supervised research by both undergraduates and graduates. I would be happy to travel to Wake Forest to visit or give a talk at your convenience. I think I would like working at Wake Forest and hope you will choose me for this job.

Letters of recommendation on my behalf are being sent by Professors Sidney Gretsky and Harold Gregory of Harvard University and Professor Lawrence Haffner of the University of California at Berkeley. If I can be of further assistance, please contact me.

Sincerely,

Ethan D. Carter

Commentary: As a junior faculty member, Ethan Carter's applications will look different from those of a first-time job candidate. For example, he leads with his current position in the cover letter and includes his dissertation topic (specifying the title would have been better) in the "Education" section of his c.v. As is typical for scientists, both vita and letter are concise (publications, research interests, etc.); atypical is the use of bullets in the c.v. Because he is applying to an institution stressing undergraduate teaching, his statement of "Teaching Philosophy" is even longer than the statement of "Research Interests," and he emphasizes his undergraduate and nonspecialist teaching. Carter's reference in the letter to being at Wake Forest could be interpreted as rather perfunctory, but he got the job.

Curriculum Vitae

Ethan D. Carter

Department of Physics	00 Robinson Street
Harvard University	Apartment 00
Cambridge, MA 02138	Cambridge, MA 02138
(617) 495-1000	(617) 864-0000
electronic mail: carter@physics.harvard.edu	

CURRENT POSITION

Harvard University   1990-present
Associate Professor of Physics, 1993-present
Assistant Professor of Physics, 1990-1993
SSC Fellow at junior faculty level, 1990-1992

EDUCATION

University of California at Berkeley   1988-1990
Miller Research Fellow at the Miller Institute
for Basic Research in Science

Harvard University   1984-1988
Ph.D. in Physics, June 1988 (specializing in high energy
    particle theory, Sheldon Glashow, adviser)
M.A. in Physics, March 1987

Michigan State University   1980-1984
B.S. in Physics, March 1984

TEACHING EXPERIENCE

Harvard University, Assistant & Associate Professor, 1991-present
- Taught undergraduate course in mechanics to AP students
- Taught graduate courses in electrodynamics, group theory,
  and astrophysics and cosmology
- Directed research of undergraduate student
- Supervised research of four doctoral students
- Supervised graduate students in advanced field theory study

Harvard University, Head Teaching Fellow, 1987-1988
- Taught sections in physics overview course for nonscientists
- Coordinated work of four other teaching fellows
- Performed administrative duties for class (114 students)
- Substituted for professor in his absence

Michigan State University, Teaching Assistant
- Led sections in trigonometry and calculus classes
- Tutored students in trigonometry and calculus

AWARDS

Sloan Foundation Fellowship, 1993-1995

SSC Fellow at junior faculty level, 1990-1992

Miller Research Fellow, 1988-1990

Graduate School of Arts and Sciences Fellowship, 1987-1988
- One of ten recipients in Graduate School of Arts and Sciences

National Science Foundation Fellowship, 1984-1987

Putnam Mathematical Competition (nationwide)
- Putnam Fellow (top five in U.S.), 1980, 1982, 1983
- Honorable mention, 1981

Harvard Fellowship Prize, 1980 (one awarded each year)

National Merit Scholar, 1980-1984

National High School Mathematics Olympiad
- Second Place, 1979

PUBLICATIONS

[One page of 23 publications appended in the original is not included here.]

RESEARCH INTERESTS

My research covers a wide variety of topics including both particle phenomenology and astrophysics. I believe that, for the next decade or so, astrophysics will dominate discoveries in particle physics, since there are very few opportunities at high energy colliders for new discoveries.

Two of my recent papers have focused on the conversion of pseudoscalars into photons in the presence of large-scale or strong magnetic fields. Such conversions may well provide the best limits on pseudoscalar couplings. Up to now, I have focused on methods which rely on the galactic magnetic field and, consequently, are sensitive only to massless pseudoscalars. I hope to use some of the same ideas in the context of stellar magnetic fields, allowing the probing of much larger masses. I hope to improve limits on the axion by this technique.

One area I have focused on recently is the possibility of a naturally small cosmological constant. A positive cosmological constant could help resolve the apparent discrepancy between the large estimated ages of stars in globular clusters and the rather large value of the Hubble constant coming from most recent experiments. It is difficult to see how such a small cosmological constant could arise. In a paper with W.D. Garretson, I explored the possibility that the universe might have a zero cosmological constant in the true vacuum, but that we might lie in a false vacuum. The smallness of the splitting between the two vacua could arise due to the appearance of an accidental discrete symmetry connecting the two vacua. The splitting would be the result of Planck-scale suppressed nonrenormalizable terms which would violate the discrete symmetry. I hope to explore models which demonstrate these ideas in a more natural way in the near future.

Neutrino physics is another area I am interested in. I have written several papers involving various neutrino mass-generation mechanisms, and I am currently getting interested in this subject once more. Neutrino masses naturally arise in many extensions of the standard model and could have important cosmological consequences. With new results from various solar neutrino and terrestrial neutrino experiments, as well as the appearance of new detectors in the near future, this will be a rapidly growing field.

Overall, I believe astroparticle physics to be one of the most promising areas in particle phenomenology in the next decade or two. I expect my research will continue to focus in this productive area.

TEACHING PHILOSOPHY

It is often said that the best way to learn material is to teach it. If this is true, then the best teacher is the one who makes the students teach what they are learning. This is my philosophy of teaching. There are many ways of implementing this idea, and I have applied several of them in my classes.

In graduate classes, I encourage students to teach one lecture on the topic of their choice. The process of organizing a lecture requires that students understand the material very well, unlike a standard assignment which emphasizes the ability to look up and use equations. Furthermore, because a teaching assignment is open-ended, it encourages them to delve deeper into the subject, rather than learning just enough to solve the problems. Finally, it encourages them to anticipate and prepare for questions, thereby questioning and strengthening their own understanding. Overall, preparing for a lecture gives them better preparation for what they will encounter as graduates than doing a homework assignment.

In my current undergraduate class, a large lecture on mechanics, having students teach the class is impractical. However, several mechanisms help students gain experience with teaching. First, I encourage students to work in study groups. This allows them to argue, discuss, and explain things to each other, forcing them to have a deeper understanding of the subject. Second, I encourage students who ask me questions to clearly articulate what they do understand. This often reveals a misconception lying at the root of their understanding, which can then be fixed. Once students see their underlying misconception, they can often solve their own problems without further input from me. Third, I give homework problems that encourage students to answer as if they were teaching. Such questions start with "explain . . ." or "show that . . . ," rather than "calculate . . ." or "find the equation . . ."

In the future, I hope to use these ideas more extensively in undergraduate classes. For example, in a small class, it would be possible to have students give a lecture or at least a short presentation. Preparing to teach promotes interaction of students with the professor in a one-on-one setting. Having the problems that are worked on by a whole class or small groups promotes camaraderie and teaching skills. Having students teach each other encourages cooperation rather than competition.

Overall, I feel that teaching by getting students to teach, or at least perform teaching-style activities, is the best way to assure a deep understanding of the material. As students learn to teach, they gain both a deep knowledge of the subject and skills that will be valuable to them in the future.

000 Longwood Avenue
Boston, Massachusetts 02115
September 26,1995

Conrad Meier, M.D.
Cullen Eye Institute
Baylor College of Medicine
Houston, TX 77030

Dear Dr. Meier:

I am writing to apply for the tenure-track faculty position in the Department of Ophthalmology at Baylor College of Medicine.

My research interest is molecular mechanisms of viral latency, specifically that of herpes simplex virus (HSV). My doctoral work in the laboratory of Dr. Donald M. Coen focused on quantitative measurement of viral gene expression during the establishment and maintenance of latency, using quantitative RT-PCR assays which I developed for a panel of HSV genes. I have also created and characterized recombinant viruses as prototypes for neuron-specific gene therapy and as reagents for studying questions of viral mechanisms. I have collaborated on studies in viral mechanisms of drug resistance.

The course of my scientific development has not been typical. Prior to seeking a doctoral degree, I was employed for many years in the laboratory of Dr. Joanne Ingwall at Harvard Medical School, in the field of cardiac biochemistry and physiology. I started as a technician, and progressed through the position of Chief Technician to Technical Director. My functions ranged from technical to scientific to managerial. I was responsible for the organization and management of the Ingwall lab: hiring, training, and supervision of personnel; development of new biochemical, physiologic, and physical procedures; and maintenance of my own research projects, including presentations both in publications and at national meetings.

Additionally, I have acquired a great range of technical skills in the fields of biochemistry, physiology, molecular biology, and virology. These include: HPLC, enzyme analysis, electrophoresis, chromatography (and other protein purification methods), analytical use of radioisotopes, and radioimmune assays. All my research experience included work with animal models and I am familiar with small animal surgical procedures, clinical assessment methods, and appropriate tissue-harvesting techniques. In my graduate work, I developed skills and expertise in: PCR methods, RNA analyses, recombinant DNA techniques, mammalian cell tissue culture, and

BL2 procedure for safe handling of human pathogens. I also have experience with computer-assisted statistical analysis.

I believe that I have the experience, breadth of knowledge, skills, and scientific maturity to successfully develop a basic research program in the molecular pathogenesis of viral eye infections in your department. Enclosed are my curriculum vitae, list of references, summary of research interests, and copies of major publications. Thank you for considering my application.

Sincerely,

Maryanne F. Katzen, Ph.D.

[Appended references are not included here.]

[This letter was written in response to the following description:]

Position Description
HERPES SIMPLEX VIROLOGIST

The Department of Ophthalmology, Baylor College of Medicine, seeks applicants for a TENURE-TRACK FACULTY position to develop a basic research program in the molecular pathogenesis of viral eye infections. Candidates should have experience in the neurobiological factors that trigger recurrences. Applicants should send their curriculum vitae, a statement of research interests, and the names of three references to: Conrad Meier, M.D., Cullen Eye Institute, Baylor College of Medicine, Houston, TX 77030. Baylor College of Medicine is an Equal Opportunity/Affirmative Action/Equal Access Employer.

Commentary: Maryanne Katzen's c.v. is concise and simple. The dates in the margin are more common in science vitas. The concise, tailored cover letter (note the job description), "Statement of Research Interests," list of references, along with the c.v. and its appended publications, won Katzen a campus interview. Note that she directly addresses her unconventional academic path, turning it into an asset.

Curriculum Vitae

MARYANNE FELICIA KATZEN

HOME ADDRESS:
58 Open Street
Jamaica Plain, MA 02130
617-555-0000
katzen@med.harvard.edu

OFFICE ADDRESS:
Harvard Medical School
000 Longwood Avenue
Boston, MA 02115
617-432-0000

EDUCATION

1989 - 1995	Ph.D., Virology, Harvard University Division of Medical Science, 1995
	Thesis: Quantification of Herpes Simplex Virus DNA and Transcripts during Latent Infection in Mouse Trigerminal Ganglia by Reverse Transcriptase PCR
1972 - 1974	B.A., Biology, University of California at San Diego, 1974
1970 - 1972	San Diego Mesa College

RESEARCH EXPERIENCE

1983 - 1989	Technical Director, Bioanalytical Laboratory, Nuclear Magnetic Resonance Laboratory, Harvard Medical School, 221 Longwood Avenue, Boston, MA
1977 - 1983	Chief Technician, Cardiovascular Division, Department of Medicine, Brigham and Women's Hospital, and Peter Bent Brigham Hospital, Boston, MA
1975 - 1976	Staff Research Associate, Cardiology Division, Department of Medicine, University of California at San Diego, La Jolla, CA

AWARDS

1994 - 1995	Albert J. Ryan Fellowship
1972 - 1974	California State Scholarship
1972	U.S. Public Health Service Pre-Medical Traineeship Award

[A page of eleven publications originally appended is not included here.]

Maryanne F. Katzen
Statement of Research Interests

Broadly, I am interested in molecular biology of gene expression in response to disease in a whole-animal, physiologic context. My early work in the laboratory of Dr. Joanne S. Ingwall focused on the energetics of heart muscle, especially as it pertained to development and progressive disease. We characterized the creatine kinase (CK) system in animal models, showing that the relative presence of isoenzymes (BB, MB, and MM) in hearts was developmentally staged and that experimentally induced hypertrophy was accompanied by re-emergence of a more fetal-like creatine kinase isozyme profile. In our animal studies we found very little MB CK in healthy adult myocardium. In diseased human myocardium we measured high levels of MB CK. Clinically, a strong correlation of elevated MB CK in blood with acute myocardial infarction (MI) had been established and provided a reliable diagnostic marker. When "normal" adult human heart tissue became available to us (obtained from autopsies of accident victims) we demonstrated that some percent of healthy adult human hearts contained very little MB CK, consistent with the various healthy adult animal models. This finding suggested that in some people an MI may occur with no consequent elevation in blood MB CK, and had direct relevance to clinical diagnosis.

Upon entering graduate school to pursue an independent academic career, I looked for a thesis lab in which I could learn molecular biology approaches and apply these methods, and my previous training in quantitative analysis, to a relevant physiologic model of disease. I found these features in the study of herpes simplex virus (HSV) latency in the mouse eye model. When I joined Dr. Coen's lab, my first project was to design, construct, and characterize a replication-defective HSV gene delivery vector. The virus which I created, tkLTRZl, is a successful prototype for a gene-delivery vehicle. It is currently being used by ourselves and others as a prototype for *in vivo* studies of viral gene expression in latency, molecular biology of pain, and immunity in the nervous system; as a reagent for tracing viral infiltration of the nervous system in blood brain barrier studies and axonal transport studies; and as a reagent for recombinant virus selection. I have created additional recombinant viruses as reagents to address questions of regulation of gene expression in latency. My thesis work focused on the expression of genes during establishment and maintenance of HSV latency in mouse trigeminal ganglia. For this I developed a sensitive, quantitative PCR approach by which several viral gene sequences could be measured for each individual infected ganglion. To improve sensitivity of detection, I developed a method for the optimization of PCR using enhancing agents which is now published in the most recent supplement of *Current Protocols in Molecular Biology*. In these studies I showed that RNA from the immediate early gene encoding ICP4, and the early gene encoding thymidine kinase, is present at low levels in latently infected ganglia and that the amount of ICP4 RNA correlates with the amount of thymidine kinase RNA (Katzen and Coen, 1995, *J. Virol.* 69:1389). These findings suggest the possibility of transactivation of the tk gene by the product of the ICP4 gene at levels which do not necessarily initiate or ensure the complex, ordered progression of productive infection referred to as the lytic cascade, but which may provide a state of reactivation readiness. In more recent studies I detailed the time course of viral DNA and RNA accumulation in mouse ganglia. In acute infection by a mutant virus which contains a deletion in the coding region of thymidine kinase, I observed a defect in late gene transcription, which implies a block at the level of viral replication. Furthermore, the RNA profile of the mutant reflects the profile of wild type virus in latency, suggesting a block in replication during latency.

In the future I would like to continue to investigate the molecular and cellular mechanisms of viral latency. I would use the mouse eye model of HSV latency to explore the following set of questions. 1A) To what extent do neurons productively infected with HSV die? To address this question, I would first quantify the relationship between PFU and copy number using plaque assays and quantitative PCR. Next I would design, construct, and characterize a recombinant virus as a reagent with which lasting evidence of maximal late gene expression, indicative of productive infection, could be detected, by, for example, expression of a cellular structural component with a unique marker such as an antigenic tag under the control of a late gene promoter. 1B) If productively infected neurons die, by what mechanism(s)? To distinguish between cytopathic effect, cell mediated lysis, and apoptosis, I envision developing a multiplex PCR diagnostic assay for determining relative levels of cell-type- and function-specific gene expression in cells "marked" with the recombinant virus described in question 1A. 1C) If there are surviving neurons which had sustained some level of productive infection, how is replication halted? Here a cellular component is probably involved, and I would pursue this question using subtractive techniques and differential display PCR methods. 2) How is progeny virus and excessive viral DNA cleared? To address this question, I would examine the role of the cells which surround neurons, the capsular cells, using histology and *in situ* PCR approaches. I have already developed quantitative PCR assays for HSV genes, and I would like to establish an *in situ* PCR protocol. 3A) Does LAT (the abundantly expressed latency associated transcript) play a role in cell death or protection from cell death during acute infection? I would want to quantify the relation between LAT expression and late-gene expression using the reagent described above and one with an additional mutation in the LAT promoter. 3B) If LAT plays a role, is it related to copy number control? Here the LAT promoter deletion mutant would be assayed using *in situ* PCR.

Beyond these HSV-specific questions, I also have a keen interest in other latent viruses, and newly-emerging viruses, and would seek productive collaborations with other virologists, specifically to quantify low levels of viral genomes and gene expression by quantitative PCR methods similar to those which I have developed for HSV genes.

Chapter Five

The Interview Process

The interview process, whether as complicated as a campus visit or as simple as a phone call, is essentially a "mutual exploration of fit." It provides both search committees and candidates with the opportunity to evaluate the potential match in greater depth, generally through personal interactions. In the anxiety of trying to market yourself and get a job, don't overlook your need to assess whether a particular environment will enable you to thrive professionally, at least for the initial stage of your career. Although this phase of the search process is grueling and stressful, you can take some comfort from the fact that the search committee is now looking for reasons to select—rather than to reject—you.

After the search committee members have completed their initial screening, they will decide on the applicants they would like to interview. Preliminary interviews in most disciplines in the humanities and social sciences are conducted at the annual professional meetings, which generally are held from November to February; between ten and twenty applicants usually are invited to interview (the *long* "short list"). Two to four will be selected from this pool and invited for campus visits. Some disciplines (e.g., political science, mathematics, and the natural sciences) and some institutions narrow the field down without the benefit of screening interviews, in which case they may bring a larger number of candidates (up to six) to campus. In an era of tight budgets, however, some departments screen candidates by telephone and many limit the number of campus visits to two or three, sometimes starting with their preferred candidate, to shorten the process.

Post-Application Procedures

You have decided which jobs to apply for, you have sent your letters and c.v., and you have arranged for your dossier or letters of recommendation to be forwarded. Your applications are in the mail by the stated deadline. Although most departments will send you a letter or a card to acknowledge the receipt of your materials, you may include a self-addressed, stamped postcard for this purpose.

Now what? You wait, and while you wait, you prepare yourself for interviews. You also keep in touch with professors and otherwise stay alert to new job openings. If your advisers are willing to phone colleagues at the institutions you most want to hire you, an enthusiastic "I really encourage you to take a close look at ___, because . . ." can be effective in moving you into the interview pile. However, some professors caution against such interventions or feel uncomfortable making them.

Don't forget to tend to your personal life as well. If anything, increase the time you devote to stress reduction activities. One recent economics job market candidate also advises that you build up a lot of "time-capital" with your spouse or significant other before your search begins: "I thought that as soon as the job search was over, life would return to normal. But after I accepted the job offer, it was time for the final push to finish the thesis. I think it will take a year of my cooking dinner every night before I'm out of debt to my wife!"[1]

In any job search, unfortunately, no news is generally bad news. The hiring institutions will concentrate their energies on scheduling the candidates they favor; negative responses come slowly, if ever. If you have heard nothing a month or more after the deadline, by all means call to inquire about the status of your application. It can't hurt; they may simply be disorganized, and a call demonstrates your interest and assertiveness.

What if you do not have any interviews scheduled by the time the convention takes place? If you are not delivering a paper, should you go anyway? If you can afford the time and the expense, the convention provides a good opportunity to continue networking, to

1. Letter to author, May 1997.

let people know that you are on the market, and to keep an eye out for any last-minute job listings or interviews that may be held there. Whether or not you have interviews already scheduled, you should get hold of a program early, plan which sessions you want to attend, and try to set up brief meetings with professors whose work particularly interests you.

Preparing for Interviews

If you do get an interview, take a moment to cheer; then roll up your sleeves for the crucial work of preparing. The advice in this section is geared primarily to the preliminary interviews, although it is applicable to all interviews. See the "Extended or Campus Interview" section on p. 118 for considerations specific to the campus interview.

First, a word about scheduling: If you have any choice about scheduling, consider the following factors in descending order of importance:

- Your convention schedule. Leave ample time between engagements such as conferences and presentations. It always takes longer than you expect to navigate the crowds.

- Your own biological rhythms. At what time of day are you at your best?

- Other strategic considerations. Strategic scheduling includes factors such as when the committee members will be freshest and most focused and how the order of interviewing will affect their memory of you. For example, one successful candidate advises avoiding late afternoon interviews, if possible. But if that's when your interview is, find a way to energize everyone.

Institutional Preparation: You will want to do some background research on the school and the department, and you will need to be prepared to describe concisely your own qualifications. Do not give short shrift to this stage of preparation! You will be interviewed for thirty to forty-five minutes; the more qualified, personable, and prepared you appear, the more likely you are to be invited for a campus interview. Put yourself in the search committee's shoes: they are trying to hire a colleague who shows "promise," i.e., someone who will bring future credit to the institution, can fill the scholarly, teaching, and administrative needs of the department, and will fit with the institutional culture—in a word, someone "tenureable."

Here is a possible "research agenda." You will undoubtedly research more thoroughly for a campus interview than for a preliminary one.

- Learn as much as you can about each institution through its catalog and Internet site, from your advisers and colleagues, and even from the college guidebooks written for high school applicants. The Office of Career Services Reading Room has many college catalogs (some in print and all on microfiche), but Web home pages often have more information, such as course syllabi and college newspapers.

- Canvass your personal network to discover any inside information, such as what the departmental politics are like, what the search committee "really" is looking for, and whether there is a strong inside candidate.

- Find out the size and "cast" of the department and how it fits into the overall structure of the institution, as well as how it relates to your discipline as a whole.

- Do some research on the individual faculty members, including their Ph.D. institutions, the general nature of their research and publications, and their tenure status.

- Study the current catalogs—and, if possible, those from previous years—to see how your teaching interests complement and support their course offerings.

Dissertation and Future Research: Develop and practice delivering short descriptions of your dissertation; these should be little two- to four-minute gems that describe the essence and the importance of your work in a way that excites your audience and entices them to ask for more (which you will, of course, be prepared to supply). Remember that you will be addressing nonspecialists. Be prepared to defend your assumptions and methodology, compare your work with that of others in the discipline and related ones, and apply your research to a current problem or issue. You should also be prepared to discuss your future research goals, framing them in terms of how they could make you a valuable addition to the department. How will your research intersect with your colleagues' interests? How can your future research plans enhance your teaching? Candidates for foreign language and literature fields also should prepare to discuss their dissertation and future research in the language of their field. Some veterans advise having several versions of your dissertation, which you deliver depending on the circumstances—the one-minute, the four-minute, the ten-minute, etc. Professor Mark Kishlansky of the History Department also suggests personalizing this discussion by telling an anecdote that explains your choice of topic and your continuing passion for it.

Teaching: To prepare for questions about teaching, think about your teaching methods, philosophy, and goals, and be prepared to discuss them, basing your discussion as much as possible on your actual experience. Develop ideas for at least one introductory lecture course, one upper-level course and/or seminar, and (if appropriate) one graduate-level course. Try to formulate sample course descriptions and syllabi or at least to consider the structure and main resources for the courses. (For courses that rely heavily on introductory or language texts, try to familiarize yourself with the primary alternatives and be prepared to defend a choice.) In most schools you will need to demonstrate breadth and flexibility in teaching expertise; you also will want to tailor your presentation to the school that will be interviewing you. If the school has an intensive freshman writing series, for example, propose something that fits into that program. You may want to speculate about courses that you would like to teach in the future, even if you could not teach them now.

Other Questions: Interviewers often touch on discipline-related issues of substance or methodology, so think about where you stand on these. Worry less about taking a position that might offend someone than about tactfully phrasing and supporting your position. Some additional questions that GSAS students have fielded include: Who do you think is doing the most exciting work in our field today? What graduate programs would you recommend to a bright undergraduate in our field?

Although they are the exception, it is always prudent to anticipate tricky, illegal, or hostile questions. By preparing, you can minimize the potential for a flustered and/or damaging response. Think about your potential weaknesses from the point of view of the search committee and how you can reassure them without sacrificing your integrity. Focus on your strengths and on how you are constructively dealing with "deficiencies" (if they really exist) and what you can bring to the department to make up for them. For example, what experiences might compensate for limited formal teaching experience? (Even if you have extensive experience, interviewers often like to challenge the relevance of teaching Harvard students for teaching their own students.)

Also try to imagine and then address the concerns underlying the questions. Moreover, if the information they are seeking is helpful to your candidacy, answer forthrightly and even volunteer information that is illegal to ask. For example, if they are trying to inquire about a trailing spouse and your spouse is very mobile, you might want to mention this, explaining why this would be a good move for both of you. In doing so, you have also answered the unspoken fear that you might not accept an offer because of your spouse. If you have concerns about the impact of a disability on your candidacy, you should anticipate unspoken concerns and take the lead in addressing your ability to perform the job.

Answers become much trickier when the information is potentially damaging. Many women wonder about how to handle subtle or not so subtle probes about their family plans. (These are more likely to surface during the campus visit.) Although such questions are illegal, it is better to answer generally and address the underlying concern than to remain silent or challenge them. For example: "My husband and I haven't made those decisions yet, but I can assure you that we are both dedicated to our own and each other's careers, no matter what decisions we make." A slightly riskier response is to ask them, in a matter-of-fact, friendly tone, how this question is relevant to the job.

The manner in which you respond is at least as important as what you say. Practice remaining calm, nondefensive (even "expansive"[2]), reasonable, and graceful. Sometimes light humor is the most effective response to a hostile or embarrassing question.

Your Questions: Finally, be sure to prepare questions for your interviewers. At this stage, you will want to ask questions about their expectations, program, or institution that show some initial knowledge of their community and a desire to contribute to it. History Professor Mark Kishlansky distinguishes between "you questions" and "me questions"; you will have plenty of time on the campus visit and even beyond for the latter. Pertinent "you" questions might address the courses they need taught; the relative emphasis on and department support for teaching and research; the tenure process (but only in the most general terms, such as the percentage of junior faculty who are tenured); the library, studio, and research facilities; the number and caliber of the undergraduate majors; the average class size; the relationship between undergraduate and graduate programs; or any unusual aspects of the department program. Postpone questions about salary or other benefits *at least* until the campus visit. Always end with a question about when they expect to have made the decision about the next round.

You are strongly encouraged to do at least one mock interview. Several departments now offer their candidates this invaluable practice. If you can't get one through your department, or if you feel particularly insecure about interviewing, you can arrange a videotaped mock interview at the Office of Career Services. You will be asked to submit your c.v. and a copy of the job description in advance to a Ph.D. counselor. During the mock interview, you will be asked typical interview questions for about thirty minutes, and then you will view the tape and discuss it with the counselor. Providing your own tape allows you to review your interview again with your

2. This is another Kishlansky term (conversation with author). Professor Kishlansky points out that the committee will remember your affect long after they've forgotten the specific response, and that it is important to appear as though you have something to learn from the interviewers.

advisers and colleagues. Mock interviews give you invaluable feedback and practice, and make you both better prepared and more self-confident for the actual interview.

Practical Preparations: Here are some practical suggestions that job candidates have offered.

- Bring plenty of extra c.v.'s, writing samples, and other materials. Arm any of your own attending faculty with a two-minute description of your field and dissertation. Don't forget to bring your correspondence with institutions with which you already have interviews.

- Take carryon luggage only.

- Bring walking shoes (or boots for winter conditions) if you have to walk between hotels.

- Bring aspirin, sleeping aids, needle and thread, or anything you need for minor emergencies and for a good night's sleep.

Dress: You should dress professionally, comfortably, and in clothes that make you feel attractive. If anything, err on the conservative side. This means, for women, a suit (a skirt suit is probably safer than pants), a skirt and jacket, or a simple dress and jacket, and, for men, trousers and sport jacket or a casual suit. Dressing in layers makes sense to combat wildly differing temperatures. Women should avoid low necklines, too-short hems, ostentatious jewelry, and overpowering perfume. Wear your "interview suit" a couple of times before you actually interview in it. You can get an idea of the appropriate attire by noting what visiting lecturers and candidates for jobs at Harvard wear when they give their presentations; everyday faculty attire may be too casual. Make sure that your clothes are clean, pressed, and mended, and that your shoes are polished.

The Preliminary or Conference Interview

Conference Logistics: As soon as you have decided to attend the conference, make your travel plans and reserve a room, preferably at the same hotel where the convention will be held. (Rooms get booked well in advance.) Conference hotels usually offer reduced rates for conventions. Although you can sometimes save money by sharing a room with friends, it's probably better not to skimp in this way; you may be glad for the peace and privacy of your own room.

Under the best of conditions, conferences are chaotic and exhausting events, so be sure to arrive early enough to rest and get your bearings before the interviews begin. It is common sense to get plenty of sleep and to avoid drinking too much alcohol or coffee.

Remember that your professors are an invaluable source of both formal and informal networking on your behalf. If your advisers (or any other faculty) are present at the convention, make sure they know your room and telephone number, and give them a copy of your c.v. (or "talking points"), if they do not already have one. At the very least, try to have a friend or mentor to call on for emotional support and advice if the going gets rough.

Check in at the information and message center upon arriving and frequently thereafter, to get information on new job listings and interview locations, pick up any messages, and generally "psych out" the system. If there is any confusion in your mind, call to confirm the time and location of each of your interviews, and leave your own room and phone number. (Otherwise leave this information in writing, in order to spare the hassled search committee chair.) If you are unable to reach interviewers by phone, seek them out in their rooms; this can make the difference in getting an interview. Check out the interview rooms ahead of time.

The Interview: Your interview will probably be held in a hotel room or suite, and there may be several faculty members present. But it may also take place in a noisy cubicle in a large room, so be prepared for both situations. Plan to arrive early (factoring in long elevator waits) to allow time both for reviewing your notes and for centering yourself with some deep breathing and the self-assurance that you have a lot to offer. Try to let go of any vestiges of the "supplicant mentality" typical of many graduate students, and, without being arrogant, step into the role of potential colleague.

As you enter the room, shake each person's hand firmly and

confidently, and greet each interviewer using his or her name (last names are safer, unless you know a person personally or the interviewers indicate otherwise). It is important to make eye contact throughout the interview with each individual as you converse.

The interviewers have presumably read your file, but do not assume that they remember the contents well. While you may need to remind them of certain elements ("as you recall, I . . ."), your essential task is to make your credentials come alive by presenting yourself as a personable, engaging, articulate, and enthusiastic candidate who has a clear sense of what you can offer them as a colleague, scholar, and teacher. The best interviews are dialogues, and you should strive for a balance in which neither you nor the interviewers dominate the conversation for too long a time. Remember, it is a "mutual exploration of fit."

After brief small talk, the typical interview begins with a query about your dissertation. (This is where the two-minute gem comes in.) Ideally, this leads to a discussion about your choice of theoretical or methodological orientation, the contribution your work makes to the field, and what your next research projects will be. Questions are often asked in critical terms, such as "Why did you choose to omit (some important material or source) from your work?" or "I'm not sure I'm convinced by your argument about . . . or methodology on . . ." Remember to respond matter-of-factly and gracefully; how you respond to such challenges and handle the discussion of controversial issues indicates to the interviewers your potential as a teacher and a colleague. If this is a research university, the interviewers will focus particularly on these research issues.

The next segment of the interview is generally devoted to questions about teaching interests and qualifications, as discussed above. (In a teaching college, it may come first.) Remember to gear your discussion to their particular institution and don't hesitate to ask questions to clarify their needs. Also bear in mind that, particularly in smaller institutions, search committees are looking for versatility, so be open to the possibility of filling teaching needs outside your specialization. Remember that you can almost always learn enough about a subject to teach an introductory course! This is a good time to inquire about collaborative teaching if it appeals to you.

If there is time, they may ask you about your concerns or elicit your questions, which you have prepared for and which may also grow out of the discussion. Don't forget to ask when you can expect to hear from them. Depending on your instincts, you may want to close with some comment about your enthusiasm for this position and why you see it as a good match.

In general, take your time to formulate answers, but be concise and to the point in your responses (without being overly terse). Beware of filling silence with chatter. At the same time, avoid appearing too controlled and "canned"; rather, try to appear spontaneous, enthusiastic, and energetic. This will happen naturally if you are engaged in the process, instead of worrying too much about how you are doing or what you should be doing. This will also enable you to be sensitive and responsive to their body language and other nonverbal cues.

Be friendly and relaxed, but focused; never lose sight of why you are there. If you find yourself with inexperienced interviewers, you may have to take some control over the interview process in order to communicate the essential information. For example, if you are bogged down on some tangential issues or unimportant details, you might say something like "I would love to discuss this further at another time, but I want to be sure I have a chance to talk/ask/find out about . . ." Finally, strive to leave them with some memorable positive impression; after all, they are unlikely to invite you back if they can't remember you five candidates later.

At the conclusion of the interview, shake hands with everyone again. As soon as you can, take a few moments to write down your impressions of the interview—observations about the interviewers, the gist of the discussion, what they seemed interested in or concerned about, unexpected questions, what you did and didn't like about your responses, and what you might do differently next time. According to Government Department Professor James Alt, "You almost always blow the first interview, so, if you have any choice, get it out of the way, not at your favorite place." This is not necessarily true, but if you do feel you've blown it, go easy on yourself and remember that mishaps and "blown interviews" have still led to campus visits! Kennedy School of Government Assistant Professor

Jeff Liebman, while not exactly botching his interviews, had a bad cold, broke his glasses, and got no sleep before his first interviews at the American Economics Association meetings and, nonetheless, received several campus "fly-backs."

After you return home, consider writing a thank-you note to the chair of the search committee. Opinions vary on the importance or even desirability of thank-you notes after the convention interview. Writing gives you the opportunity to reiterate your interest in the position and enthusiasm for their department, and also to add information or to correct a misimpression if you need to. But better not to write at all if it comes across as gratuitous or even "groveling."

The Extended or Campus Interview

The campus visit (or "fly-back") can be seen as the apex of the job-search process, not only in its intensity and importance but also because it marks a new stage in the psychology of the job search. By the time you are invited for a campus visit, the committee (or a significant portion of it) has coalesced behind your candidacy—along with that of one to five other candidates. They are now looking for reasons to hire you, not to eliminate you. While this notably warms the atmosphere, the campus visit is nonetheless a grueling experience, because you are constantly "on stage" for a period of one to two days. The jam-packed schedule usually includes interviews with faculty, students, and a dean and/or another administrator; the crucial job talk and perhaps a practice teaching session; and lunches, dinners, and other deceptively casual social events.

As earlier in the job-search process, the key ingredients to success in the campus interview are thorough preparation and a confident psychological stance: you want to be your professional, enthusiastic "best" self without worrying too much about the outcome. Remember that while this is a mutual exploration of fit, you also want to convey that you take your interviewers seriously and will be a good colleague, community member, and friend. Indeed, the unspoken agenda of the department members and search committee at this stage is to get a good sense of the "personal fit."

Logistics and Preparation: The invitation usually comes by telephone from the chair of the department or the search committee, usually within a week to a month of the convention meeting. You may be asked to submit more information or materials. Ask the chair or whoever calls you to be very explicit about the schedule, including whom you will meet with, and about the conditions of the job talk. For example, what would they like in the way of content, length, and questions? Who exactly will be in the audience? Will you have access to special equipment that you may need? What is the size of the room? If you have any choice about timing, make your preferences known. Psychology Professor Stephen Kosslyn advises giving the talk before your interviews with faculty, presumably to provide grist for conversation and a chance to clarify and amplify your talk. In any case, ask them to schedule in breaks for you, especially before your job talk and/or teaching; you don't want to have to manufacture bathroom breaks in order to catch your breath. You will probably be informed about reimbursement arrangements; if not, you should by all means inquire. Finally, don't hesitate to call the person you have been dealing with and/or the department secretary to clarify any details and perhaps get a written schedule.

Ordinarily, all or part of your travel and accommodation expenses are paid by the school. You frequently have to pay your travel expenses up-front, so be sure you have a credit card to tide you over until you are reimbursed, and *be sure* to keep all your receipts. Guest accommodations may be provided on campus, or you may be lodged in a nearby hotel. Don't be surprised if they ask you to stay over a Saturday night to save on plane fare. In general, try to be as flexible as possible without compromising your own legitimate needs, keeping in mind their difficulties in scheduling multiple candidates. Consider arriving a day early if you are traveling across time zones or are concerned about flight cancellations and weather problems.

Preparation is even more important at this stage than for the convention interview. For general preparation, go to the job talks given by candidates interviewing for jobs in your own department, and notice what seems to work and not work (both from your own reactions and those of faculty). For preparation specific to the campus, go back to the catalogs, library databases (such as HOLLIS), and the institution's own World Wide Web site, as well as to anyone in your professional network as sources of information. For sample questions, refer to the "Preparing for Interviews" section above. Bring plenty of copies of your vita, course syllabi, and job-talk handouts.

It is important to consider the character and mission of the institution and how you might fit in there. For example, if it is a women's college, what is your opinion on single-sex education? If it is a denominational college, could you contribute to that mission? How would you do as a humanist at a technical university or as a scientist at a college which stresses the humanities? This preparation will help you to formulate questions to ask, to think more about your possible contributions to the institution's and the department's needs, and to be more alert to potential pitfalls. During your visit, it will also allow you to convincingly demonstrate your interest and enthusiasm for the faculty and students and their college and community.

As noted above, there are three main elements of the campus visit: (1) the series of interviews, (2) the job talk/seminar and/or a teaching demonstration, and (3) social occasions. Because you will be constantly "on show," you will need to keep your guard up, while at the same time appearing natural and spontaneous. One rueful candidate recalled an interview at a university where a friend from graduate school was now an assistant professor. She confessed to him her doubts about her ability to teach a course totally outside her specialty, despite her assurances to the committee; this quickly made its way back to the committee and may have cost her the job.

Interviews: You may be scheduled for a series of individual interviews with members of the department and the department chair. These discussions are designed to evaluate you as a potential colleague. Try to meet with any senior faculty who won't be at your job talk, so they will have some idea of you and your work. Be prepared to discuss your current and future research, as well as issues related to teaching, the curriculum, the student body, and the trends and controversies of your field. You may be asked the same or similar questions by different interviewers but you can avoid the "broken-record syndrome" if you engage with each person as an individual, asking questions about his or her work, and trying to make connections with your own interests. (Your preliminary research on the faculty should have given you a general idea of their areas of interest; however, you need not have read their work, except, of course, for people in your own subfield. In fact, some faculty report being turned off by what they regard as excessive preparation.)

You, in turn, should have come up with a number of questions about issues important to you. Asking the same or similar questions of a number of faculty members affords you a variety of perspectives. Ask faculty members about their futures: What do the department and school value when making tenure decisions? Are they teaching courses that they enjoy, and is the course load satisfactory? Do they get the time and support necessary to continue their own research? (This would include support for summer research, conference travel, and research assistants, as well as funds for laboratory equipment, computers and software, library materials, and other discipline-specific resources.) You will want to get a sense of the department "culture," i.e., how faculty members relate to each other, their students, and the rest of the institution. What roles do faculty, and particularly junior faculty, have in addition to teaching and research? Will you be expected to participate in advising, campus governance, or community service? Professor James Alt of the Government Department suggests asking each faculty member you speak with, "What are the two or three best and worst things about working here?"

One difficulty you may encounter while interviewing is the "H-Factor"—the stereotype that you would only be interested in working in an institution like Harvard, and that if hired by a "second-string" school, you would "trade up" at the first opportunity. You will need to affirm your genuine interest in the school, particularly if you are applying for a position at one with a different mission or focus than Harvard's. It will help to overcome shyness, which might be interpreted as arrogance, and ask questions—and really listen to the answers.

Another potential pitfall is engaging in criticism of your home institution; no matter what your experience has been, resist the temptation (and faculty often will try to tempt you) to criticize or gossip about colleagues and the institution. If someone, even if it is the department chairman, makes a disparaging remark about a colleague, at Harvard or elsewhere, deftly turn the conversation in a different direction: "That's not been my experience, fortunately. By the way . . ." or "I wouldn't know about that . . ." If the remark refers to your adviser, you probably want to make a stronger statement of support, if you can in good conscience.

As in preliminary interviews, you can avoid other land mines by anticipating potentially difficult or illegal questions and having a response in mind. Two general principles for handling such questions are (1) try to put yourself in your interviewers' shoes and imagine what the concern behind the question is, and then address the concern, and (2) answer forthrightly if the information they are seeking is helpful to your candidacy.

Non-U.S. citizens might have to field a question regarding their visa status. You must be forthcoming about your status, but most colleges and universities are used to hiring foreign nationals and can make the case for unique qualifications. However, if you do not have an H-2 visa (green card), you might help your cause—particularly at a small college that lacks institutionalized mechanisms—by indicating that you are familiar with the process and willing to help it along. This requires having done your homework with the International Office at Harvard and perhaps an outside lawyer.

Gay, lesbian, and bisexual job seekers have wondered about whether to come out of the closet, particularly in response to questions regarding family. There is no easy answer. Options range from being completely open (e.g., in their c.v.'s) to never volunteering the information, depending on the candidate's own level of comfort. Candidates have engaged the chairman or the dean in conversation about diversity policy as a prelude to specific questions about the environment for gay men and lesbians. Some people have done preliminary research trying to ascertain how hospitable the institution and community are; they have suggested looking up community resources in the *Gayellow Pages* or a gay travel guide (e.g., Damron) and contacting relevant student or staff organizations on campus to get information and the names of gay or lesbian faculty members they might call. The Internet also contains a wealth of helpful resources. In the end, the truism may bear repeating that if you are deterred from talking about yourself by the atmosphere in an institution or if you are rejected for a job on the basis of your orientation, chances are that it is not a good fit for you.

Instead of individual interviews with faculty, you may have one or more group interviews. The advice for similar interviews at the annual meetings holds for campus visits. The main things to remember are

- to include all the members of the group in your responses and with your body language,

- to strive for a conversation rather than simply a question-and-answer session, and

- not to worry so much about pleasing everyone that you lose your own "voice" and come across as a pandering politician.

A meeting with students may be scheduled, and you should take it very seriously. One candidate at a small college lost his bid for the job when he was arrogant and flippant with the students. Remember that you can learn from students as well as from the faculty. Ask about their programs of study: Are they writing senior theses? Do they have plans for graduate school? A meeting with graduate students could be invaluable in evaluating the level of support for and intellectual caliber of the graduate program. Acquaint yourself with what students like and dislike about the department. One job candidate in history passed out copies of her course syllabi to grateful graduate students. These may be your students someday; it makes sense to treat them with respect.

Another item on the agenda will be a meeting with a dean and perhaps other administrators who will familiarize you with their policies and vision of the academic community as a whole. They will want to know how you will fit in as a department member and what kind of contribution you will make to the community. They will also want to ascertain whether you have leadership or administrative skills, and whether you are likely to play an active and valuable role on committees. This meeting is also an opportunity to learn about the institution's policies on promotion and tenure. There probably will be some general talk of salary and benefits, but don't press for specifics or commit yourself to any figures yet. The questions you might want to ask them should also have an institutional cast, e.g.: What are the greatest challenges and opportunities facing the college and the department? What are possibilities for interdepartmental collaboration?

A campus visit often ends with a meeting with the chair of the search committee or of the department. This will give you a chance to clarify any confusion, ask outstanding questions, and find out their search timetable and procedure for notifying you. If you are under time pressure because of other offers, now is the time to tell them. This may also be the opportunity to divulge, if you haven't earlier, that you have a dual-career situation—especially if you have a good feeling about the place and the chair may be in a position to help your spouse find a job. Some candidates prefer *not* to risk jeopardizing their chances for the offer by bringing this up, since the search committee might perceive it as an extra problem, other things being equal; they suggest waiting to raise this issue until after the offer is made. In matters like these, it is probably best to rely on your own intuition.

The Job Talk: Probably the single most important event of the visit will be your "public" job talk, which is the only common point of reference the faculty has to evaluate your understanding of the discipline, the quality of your research, and your teaching ability. It characteristically lasts from thirty minutes to an hour, with questions following. There seems to be a trend to shorter job talks, which Renée Baernstein, a history candidate, has dubbed "job talk lite." You may be asked to give a presentation on a topic of your own choice, typically a portion of your dissertation research, or to present a typical undergraduate lecture. In teaching colleges, you are sometimes asked both to give a job talk and to teach a real class.

Above all, be absolutely sure who your audience will be. More than one candidate has arrived prepared for a roomful of undergraduates only to be faced with a group of critical faculty members, or vice versa. Ideally, your talk should walk the lines between sophistication and accessibility; esoterica and generality; depth and breadth; and detail, methodology, and data, on the one hand, and the larger issues and implications, on the other. Remember that almost no one in the audience will be a specialist in your area. One way of conceptualizing the talk is as a double funnel: You begin with the broad issues and questions and some context ("This will be elementary, but let's make sure we have a common frame of reference . . ."). Then you give a lucid explanation of a limited area of your research, followed by a dazzling but *brief* technical exposition for the specialists (if there are any). To conclude, you discuss the broader implications of your work for the field or for policy or future research ("a tour of the horizon"), connecting these, if possible, to the interests of your audience. For scientists, the technical portion might be longer. Many people advise answering the question in the first five minutes, so that if your listeners' attention wanders, they still will remember the main point.

Your presentation should be clear and memorable; you want the audience to leave with two or three major points firmly lodged in their minds, feeling that they have learned something worth knowing. Using stories, examples, and metaphors is an effective technique. Visual aids—either slides or handouts—are standard in some disciplines (e.g., sciences, economics, and art). They can be an asset in most others, but only if they are error-free and if you have prepared thoroughly (e.g., if you have loaded your slides correctly). If you do use handouts, be sure you have enough and don't pass them out until just before you want people to look at them.

Strive for a lively, enthusiastic, and engaging delivery; this is much more likely if you "talk" rather than read your paper. To this end, consider writing out the presentation and then condensing it to a detailed outline. That way you will have the accurate and elegant turns of phrase in your memory but give a more natural talk. You can always read long quotes and portions where precision is paramount. Finally, if you get confused or if something goes wrong during your talk, try to resolve the problem quickly and resume your talk as calmly as possible.

The question period allows faculty to evaluate your "grace under pressure," as well as to show off a little in front of each other. With this hidden agenda in mind, be sure to treat each question seriously and courteously, even if it is "off the wall." If you don't understand a question, ask for clarification; if you can't answer a question, take some time to think about it, perhaps to frame it in a way you can answer (like you did in your oral exams). Or consider thinking about it out loud, if you think well on your feet, or simply saying that you'd like to think about it some more and come back to it. If you are asked a question that's meant to pin you to one side of a discipline debate, it is probably best to answer diplomatically but honestly and risk antagonizing one part of the group, rather than to straddle the fence and risk alienating everyone. The main thing is to maintain your self-possession and confidence (without arrogance). If humor comes lightly and easily to you, it can be an effective technique.

An excellent way to get a feel for what makes for a successful job talk is to attend the ones offered by candidates for jobs in your department. Talk to faculty members about what worked and didn't work. Even more important, of course, is to rehearse, rehearse, rehearse your own job talk before you leave! Practice it—complete with visuals—in front of your professors and peers, and even your friends and relatives. Ask for insightful, critical, tough questions and comments following your practice talk(s). These reactions are an opportunity to engage in a debate or clarification of the ideas and issues you presented. Sociology Professor Mary Waters relates how she was devastated by a question that followed her practice job talk because it uncovered a "fatal flaw" in her dissertation; fortunately, she was able to develop a counter-argument that stood her in good stead when she got the same question after her real job talk here at Harvard.

Teaching Demonstrations: As with the job talk, get precise advance information about the level and nature (lecture? seminar?) of the class you will be teaching, and whether the content will be predetermined by the professor's syllabus or will be more or less up to you to choose. In either case, prepare thoroughly, getting advice and possibly a practice session from the Bok Center on effective pedagogical techniques. Prepare handouts, slides, discussion questions, or other exercises, if appropriate. And it always helps to prepare for unexpected contingencies (e.g., misinformation from the chairman, a lethargic class, etc.). Fundamentally, however, you must rely on the confidence that comes from solid teaching experience and comfort with your own teaching style.

Informal and Social Occasions: You will be taken on campus tours and visits to the library, laboratories, and other facilities. You may be shown your future office, and be able to ascertain whether the equipment and library collections that are necessary for your research are available or will be provided. Don't be deceived by the more casual tenor of these social interactions, which are rich sources of information for both you and the hiring faculty. Although you want to exercise discretion constantly, if you are comfortable volunteering personal information, your hosts will tend to respond in kind, and the general tone of the visit can become warmer. Remember, there is much they are eager to know about you as a "whole person" but are often afraid to ask.

You may be taken on a drive around the community (and if your hosts don't offer this, it is appropriate to request it). This is an opportunity to ask about housing availability, prices, and commercial and cultural resources. Is there home mortgage assistance? What is the nature of the social life on campus and in town? What are the main attractions of living in this town and area? If you have children, you will probably want to ask about schools, but note that this inquiry leads naturally to the spousal issue. Candidates have reported faculty members both directly inquiring about family and doing so more subtly through questions about whether you would like to know about schools. Particularly in small college towns, having a family is often viewed a positive factor by the faculty, indicating a desire to settle down in the community.

Your visit will be punctuated by various social occasions—a breakfast and/or lunch, perhaps a reception, and dinner. Make sure that you talk with as many people as you can and that you are clear on their names. If you are shy, try to engage people by asking questions. On the other hand, don't be shocked if you are ignored for some period of the conversation, while faculty catch up with each other and the latest gossip. You can also learn a lot by observing the social interactions: Who socializes with whom? What is the overall atmosphere—formal or casual, tense or collegial? In social situations, be sparing in your alcohol consumption and wary of making casual observations or offhand remarks that might be misunderstood. And continue to resist the temptation to engage in gossip or criticism about Harvard. By the end of the visit, if not before, someone may have emerged as an ally, the person taking primary responsibility for

_ ___ visit or championing your candidacy. You can often elicit more information from this person, and, perhaps, raise some of your more sensitive concerns (e.g., the treatment of women, minorities, or gays on the campus). Finally, don't forget to ascertain their decision timetable and to make arrangements for reimbursement of your expenses.

Post-Visit Activities: Remember to write a thank-you letter upon your return, at least to the chair of the search committee, and, if it is a different person, probably also to the faculty member who took primary responsibility for your visit. (You may be including receipts, or, more likely, sending them separately to the department administrator.) Then focus your energies on making other campus visits (if you have them), finishing your dissertation (if you haven't already), and generating more options (if you need to). If you haven't heard from the institution(s) that you visited within a week of the date when they told you they would have a decision, by all means call to inquire about the status of the search. If you have another offer in the meantime, it is perfectly appropriate to inquire earlier than that. In some circumstances, your adviser may be willing to make a call to try to get a sense of the situation.

Delays are not unusual and may simply mean that the department is taking its time interviewing other candidates and/or that it may be waiting for final approval from the administration. On the other hand, a delay could indicate a split department or that they are waiting to hear back from another candidate to whom they have made an offer. More than one job candidate has warned against getting cocky because people on campus told you to expect an offer or that you were the best candidate.

If you are not offered the job, do *not* take it personally! Remember that many arbitrary, uncontrollable factors influence hiring decisions. If you feel comfortable doing so, it is probably worth asking the search committee directly why you didn't get the offer; occasionally you will be given truthful and valuable feedback. At the same time, receive the information skeptically, as they may simply be making up reasons to soften the blow or to justify an essentially arbitrary decision. In some cases, your adviser or another member of the department may be able to get more useful feedback. Finally, take comfort from the fact that you got this far, that you have gained invaluable experience for the next round, and that un-expected benefits can emerge from seeming "failures."

Probably the best way to get a feel for the interview process, short of going through it yourself, is to hear about the experiences of your contemporaries. In reading the story—in her words—of Sharon Lang, a recent job candidate in social and cultural anthropology, you will perhaps gain confidence in your ability to emerge successful from even the toughest of campus visits.

I received a phone call from the chair of the University of Redlands (CA) informing me that I was one of their top twelve candidates and, since they had not set up preliminary interviews at the conference, they were going to phone interview me. I had two days' notice. When they called I was on a speaker phone and there was a room full of people on the other end. Three of them rotated asking me questions and then I would rattle off some response—whatever came to mind because I had no time to find the index card with an appropriate written blurb of potential answers from the pile in front of me. I had expected that the phone interview would have been a dialogue but after my responses there would be dead silence on the other end. It only lasted thirty minutes, though they had told me it would be forty-five, and after I hung up I felt sure that I had blown it; I had the most massive headache for two days. Then I got a call from the chair (who tracked me down at my friend's house in North Carolina) telling me I had made it to the top four and they were going to fly me out!

I flew out and found my way to their alumni house where I was staying and wandered around alone—no one met me—for twenty-four hours. At 7:30 a.m. on Monday morning, I was jet lagged, stressed out, and completely exhausted. Thanks to the screaming hoards of men outside my window until 4:30 a.m., I had had about two hours of sleep. The day consisted of hourlong interviews with individual faculty members—first the chair, then the director of the interdisciplinary program, then other professors—each one would take me to the next, with no break for a coffee or to use the bathroom. (After four hours I finally asked to use the bathroom.)

I had lunch with several students and then was brought directly to the next faculty interview; at that point I could barely keep my eyes open. At 3:30 I had a break and someone picked me up twenty minutes later. I gave an hourlong presentation on my research; they had not brought water but one professor offered to get me a juice from the machine in the hall. After the talk there was a question-and-answer session for about forty minutes and then we broke. A professor gave me a lift back to the alumni house and then fifteen minutes later the chair showed up and took me to dinner at a restaurant with six others. There I had to lead an informal discussion on pedagogy, which I had been told about; in fact, it turned out to be kind of fun with everyone telling their teaching stories. My main concern throughout the day was just staying awake.

The frat rush continued the next night, and the day started all over again at a 7:45 a.m. meeting with one faculty member and then I was passed to the next. I was supposed to have a break from 10:30 to 11:00 before teaching a class but the equipment I had requested wasn't set up, so we did this then. At 11:00 a.m., thirty-five students poured in and I taught the class with the eight members of the search committee sitting in the back row and taking notes.

We went directly to lunch after the class, where I met a different group of students; then followed interviews with the dean, the president, faculty from other departments, and anyone else they could think of. It finally ended with a group interview at about 5:00 p.m. at which point it seemed that everyone was completely exhausted...

I felt sure that I did not get the job after so many mishaps during the interview: for example, the dean had asked me about philosophy professors I had during college and I could not come up with a single name, and it was in a department that had been one of my two majors! Amazingly, I got a call six days later offering me the job.[2]

2. Sharon Lang, e-mail to author, May 1997.

Part III

The Job Offer and Beyond

Chapter Six

The Job Offer

This chapter addresses the final stage of the job-search process—job offers or the lack thereof. Think positively and read the primary section on receiving and negotiating the job offer; to cover your bases, check out the second section on what to do if the offer does not materialize.

Negotiating Your First Academic Job Offer

You have just received a call from the department or search committee chair offering you a job. Congratulations! Go ahead and celebrate! But don't assume, as do many first-time academic job candidates, that once you have received a job offer, your arduous search is over. In fact, no matter how delighted you are with an offer, it is wise to view it as part of the last stage of the process—the negotiation stage, even if you ultimately decide not to negotiate anything. This section offers some general principles and advice on negotiating academic job offers, particularly initial offers for tenure-track jobs. Because negotiation etiquette and conventions vary by discipline, you are strongly encouraged to consult your dissertation and/or department placement adviser regularly during this final phase of the job search. In addition, you may want to consult *Getting to Yes* by Roger Fisher and William Ury,[1] many of whose

1. Roger Fisher and William Ury, with Bruce Patton, ed., *Getting to Yes: Negotiating Agreement Without Giving In*, 2d ed. (New York: Penguin Books, 1991).

133

principles are incorporated here. Even before you receive an offer, you can do some preliminary preparation.

Negotiable Conditions for Academic Jobs. As a first-time job candidate, you may be unaware of the range of negotiable issues, even for "entry-level" assistant professorship positions. (In general, you have less leverage and latitude in negotiating replacement and part-time jobs, although this will vary somewhat by school and circumstances, e.g., how desperate they are.) Indeed, salary may be the least significant point of negotiation, in terms both of what is possible to achieve and what will benefit you the most in your professional development. Items for discussion may include the following:

- The amount of time you'll have to decide on this offer

- Your starting date (including deferment in order to take a postdoc)

- Reduced teaching load (increasingly common for the first year)

- Lab facilities and equipment (a key element in relevant fields)

- Your own computer or easy computer access

- Money for new library resources (including films, slides, CDs)

- Summer research support

- Travel funds for conferences

- Early (or extended) sabbatical or leave (including parenting, if relevant)

- Early (or delayed) tenure review

- Extra teaching fellows or research assistants

- Extra secretarial assistance

- Office space/location

- Parking permit

- Moving expenses

- Your benefits package: health, life, disability, tuition, and retirement are the most common benefits offered and are frequently available for spouse and dependents as well. Less common benefits include on-site day care, spouse employment assistance, and a pharmaceutical plan. See whether the employer has the ability to negotiate any of these items and/ or the date when coverage begins.

- Assistance in finding and sometimes in financing housing

- Assistance in finding spousal employment

Obviously, you would not want to negotiate on all of these items, but you might want to bring the most important ones into the discussion. Bear in mind that the department chair may have little discretion in some of these areas (e.g., salary, benefits, housing) and may serve mainly as a conduit to the dean. Remember, too, that as you advance in your career and negotiate future job offers, you will have more leverage and the employer will have more latitude; in other words, more of these items are likely to be "on the table."

Preparing for Negotiation. In general, do not make requests or otherwise negotiate until you receive an offer. Meanwhile, take the time to do some background research concerning the possible offer(s).

1. *Think about **your** interests.*

- How much do you want the job?

- What kind of relations do you want with your prospective colleagues?

- How important are various negotiable aspects of the job? What is essential to you, that is, what are the conditions without which you will not accept? (Presumably you will have mentioned the essentials during your campus visit or another interview.) Set priorities. Think creatively of possible packages and tradeoffs.

- How risk-averse are you? By negotiating too aggressively, you are risking your future relations with at least the chair and/or having your bluff called; and it is even possible, though not likely, that *a job offer might be withdrawn.*

Although you will have your own priorities, former GSAS Dean Brendan Maher's advice is worth pondering: "the prime criteria for a first job are time, space, and money"[2]—enough time to do independent research and writing, space for research, and money to avoid moonlighting or teaching summer school to make ends meet. He also advises giving greater weight to the quality of the institution than to geography.

2. *Think about **their** interests.* Try to anticipate their perceptions, values, interests, and constraints. What are their alternatives?

You'll be fortunate if you have a source of inside information about the search process and competition. Otherwise, assume they have strong alternative candidates. Generally, department chairs have some flexibility in the use of department funds to cover summer research; conference funds; extra teaching fellow, research assistant, and secretarial help; and lightened teaching loads (some places grant this as a matter of course to first-year teachers). They also have some control over perks such as computer access, office space, lab facilities, and parking. Again, advance information on the norms at this particular institution or department is invaluable.

3. View the prospective negotiations as a *search for mutual gain* rather than an automatic "you win/I lose" (zero-sum) situation. The department or search committee chair is not an adversary, but a potential ally and future colleague, with whom you are likely to have many more shared goals and interests than conflicting ones. Remember, this committee and department (at least a majority) have decided that you are the best person for this job, and they not only want you to come, they want you to thrive there. You may have discussed some of your needs and concerns during the campus visit

2. Letter to author, 1993. Bear in mind that Professor Maher's field is psychology and that he was assuming the goal was a career in a probably first-class research institution.

and thus already begun the process of jointly "fleshing out" a job offer.

4. *Use objective criteria to justify your requests.* Using objective standards or principles (such as comparability, fairness, obvious need) greatly reduces the effects of personality, idiosyncrasy, and relative power in the negotiation.

5. *Find out the likely salary range* for similar positions in your field. Sources of information include your adviser or placement counselor, your professional association, the university/college itself (try the academic dean's office), or published figures. For example, the annual Almanac issue of *The Chronicle of Higher Education Almanac,* published in late August or early September and available on the Web and in the OCS Reading Room Annex, lists average full-time faculty salary figures by rank and type of institution, as well as by discipline in four-year institutions. Several other Internet sources for faculty salaries are noted in the Bibliography. *Note that salary ranges for assistant professors within a given department tend to be rather narrow and department chairs may have little or no flexibility in deviating from the established range.*

6. *Know your BATNA (Best Alternative To a Negotiated Agreement).* The possibilities are:

- You have *no good alternatives*—either no other offers or clearly inferior offers. If you are risk-averse or completely satisfied, you may not want to negotiate at all; otherwise, given that they want you to join them, there is no reason not to try. They do not need to know you have no other good options, though they may have their own ways of finding out, and you should not lie if asked directly. In any case, you intend to accept their initial offer if necessary.

- You have *one or more credible alternatives*—your choice will depend at least partly on the exact offer or package negotiated. This is an enviable position, but you need to be clear about your priorities. What conditions must be met to make this job the most attractive one?

- You have a *superior alternative.* Here you must decide whether you want to negotiate with the less preferred institution for the sole purpose of extracting a better offer from the preferred one. Obviously this is risky because people at the less-preferred school may feel used and spread the word.

7. *Consider your own strengths.* This is clearly related to calculating your BATNA, but even if you have no credible alternatives, knowing and emphasizing your strengths can be helpful, particularly when they dovetail with the particular needs of the department that may make you the offer. Bear in mind that *you will be in your strongest negotiating position during the period between receiving and accepting the offer.*

8. *Find your own style.* You may find it difficult to strike a balance between an overly passive stance, which is traditional for graduate students, and a too-aggressive one. In general, use negotiation as a problem-solving method rather than as a game or adversarial process. Adopt the style that feels right and natural to you.

The Negotiations. You will probably receive the initial offer over the phone. It is not a good idea to accept an offer immediately. But, if you feel prepared and you wish to negotiate, you can begin right then. First, however, express your pleasure at receiving the offer and your enthusiasm for their institution/department and your potential employment with them. Next, clarify any aspects of the offer as necessary. Then you might express your reservations, if you have any, and ask whether there is any possibility of obtaining, for example, additional lab facilities, library resources, or summer research support. If you do decide to negotiate salary, ask whether there is any flexibility in the figures, and be prepared to give your figure and reasons for it.

If you don't know what you want to ask for, or the offer has taken you by surprise, express your pleasure, clarify the offer, ask any informational questions you have, and say that you will get back to them after you've had a chance to think about the information.

When negotiating, it is wise to be *straightforward, matter-of-fact, and honest;* you don't have to reveal your BATNA or bottom line (though there may be circumstances where you want to), but you should never deceive in a way that would damage your credibility in the future, either in that institution or elsewhere. *Explain and justify your interests,* as you make your request(s). *Listen carefully* to get additional information on your potential employer's interests and constraints. Do not press on matters beyond their control, although you can certainly ask for some commitment to intervene with the responsible agencies, like the child care center or the housing authority. You can use any leverage you actually have (e.g., "I really want to come here, but —— has offered me x, y, and z. Is there anything you can do to make it easier to turn them down?"). How far you go beyond that will depend on you; bluffing always carries risks. Finally, silence can be an effective tool, especially in face-to-face negotiations.

In the spirit of a joint venture for mutual gain, *look for common interests* behind seemingly conflicting positions. Work with the chair to generate creative options and solutions to your different positions or even interests. For example, suppose he or she is sympathetic to your need to publish, but has no money for course reductions this year. How about more teaching assistants? Or less demanding courses? Or more summer research money? Or a reduction of administrative or departmental duties?

Or suppose you know that you will not have time to prepare courses for fall term (e.g., because you'll be too busy finishing your dissertation, or perhaps you are expecting a baby). Can you work out a semester's maternity leave? Find a substitute? Schedule all your courses—or better, a reduced load—in the second semester?

Dual-career issues can be particularly vexing. While a few institutions have established policies and procedures designed to support dual-career couples,[3] in most places the chair or even the

3. Some of these are outlined in Paul Elie, "Hiring à Deux," *Lingua Franca: The Review of Academic Life* 2, no. 3 (February/March 1992): 27-33.

dean may have little authority to create a spousal position, especially for junior faculty. In this case, the best they can offer is to put you and your spouse in touch with appropriate people inside or outside their institution. How actively they assist in this effort depends on how much they want you, as well as on the particular circumstances. You may increase their motivation by explicitly stating—or, better, strongly hinting—that a job for your spouse is a condition of your acceptance, but you had better be prepared to give up the job. Harvard job candidates have experienced both outcomes—having to turn down job offers and having an enterprising dean find a position (not necessarily tenure-track) for the trailing spouse.

Negotiations will most likely be conducted in stages, and you may introduce new requests or change your priorities during the process. But don't do this lightly, as this kind of pattern might frustrate the chair, as well as undermine your credibility. You may well decide to make a second, more low-key visit to the campus and community with your spouse or significant other, to gather more information. Throughout the process, you'll want to convey to the employer an enthusiasm for the job, the institution, and your potential employment there.

Once the negotiations are complete, reiterate the offer as you now perceive it. Ask the chair to send the offer in writing and indicate your intention to accept as soon as you receive the letter. If something is left out, stipulate it yourself in your letter of acceptance; e.g., "I understand from our earlier conversations that . . ." (You may feel awkward about pushing to have the agreement completely spelled out in writing, feeling it implies a lack of trust. History Professor Kishlansky reminds us that it is not a matter of trust, but rather to guard against both the likelihood that memories fade and the possibility that the current negotiator may not be around two or three years hence.) Also express your appreciation of his or her willingness to respond to your concerns, to go to bat for you—however you want to say it. If you are not going to accept, explain why as tactfully, honestly, and constructively as possible. Reiterate your positive impressions and your regret that the job didn't work out, and write a follow-up letter as well. In short, leave them with a positive impression of you.

The ethics of the profession dictate that once you have accepted a job offer, you are bound to that decision. Although exceptions occur, you should make the decision as though it were your final one. Once you decide, immediately inform all other potential employers, as well as your adviser(s) and anyone else who has assisted you in your job search, of your decision.

Professional ethics also require that employers give you a reasonable amount of time to make a decision. If you are waiting for other offers, "reasonable" is most likely defined by the time when most of the offers will be out in a given field (usually ranging from mid-January to mid-March). If you expect to take this offer, ask for a reasonable period to think it over—perhaps a few days or, at most, two weeks. If you feel they are putting undue pressure on you, you might ask your adviser or department placement counselor to intervene. If you are pressed for a decision on one offer before others are made, call the chair(s) from the preferred institution(s), explain your situation, and ask whether they can speed up their decision making. In addition, try to get an accurate assessment of your chances there, to maximize your information in the event you must decide on one offer before receiving any others. Increasingly, some less prestigious institutions are speeding up their hiring process in order to present desirable candidates with offers before other options are apparent. In these difficult situations, gather as much information as possible, try to generate new alternatives (e.g., a fallback one-year appointment), clarify your goals and values with someone you trust, and listen to your intuition as well as your reason. Only you can decide, however.

If You Don't Get a Job Offer

If by April or May you have not received a job offer, do not give up hope. Because fellowship awards and departures to new positions are sometimes not announced until late in the semester, some positions open up in the late spring. Faced with a late vacancy, department chairs will turn to their colleagues to get names of candidates who are available. More than once, candidates have been asked if they are still interested in a position long after they have given up hope. Perhaps the school's first-choice candidates turned them down, or the funding approval was delayed. These last-minute positions usually have a quick turnaround time as departments endeavor to meet course catalog deadlines and make decisions before graduation and the summer. Recall the stories of John Fox and Allan Fung (recounted in Chapter Three), both of whom found late-breaking jobs as a result of informal contacts.

Having read this book, you know that your job hunt might not be successful the first or even the second time around, and so you have developed contingency plans. It is crucial during this interim period to have a position that supports you and yet allows time for you to be productive in your research and writing.

Keep looking for research or part-time and replacement teaching positions in your department, the Social Studies and History and Literature programs, the Extension School, or at a good local or community college. Also check into late-deadline postdoctoral fellowships in your field. As you have heard before, the most effective technique in this situation is networking as widely as possible—through your existing contacts or by contacting GSAS alumni/ae or department chairs in selected target schools. At the very least, try to maintain or create an academic affiliation from which to launch a more credible job search, e.g., an unpaid research fellowship at a university-affiliated center or institute. You would then have to find a source of employment, but in any case, try not to accept interim employment that will prevent you from publishing and otherwise enhancing your c.v. for next year's job search.

Chapter Seven

Afterword: Getting Off to a Good Start

Congratulations on beginning your academic career! Although technically outside the purview of this guide, a brief discussion of the challenges and pitfalls of the first year of teaching may ease your transition into academe.[1] As Professor Patricia Chaput describes it in her excellent academic job-search guide for Slavic Department job candidates:

> You should know that the first year as an Assistant Professor can be a very tough year, and that while it may be exhilarating, it is not uncommon to begin to feel overwhelmed and anxious. This year is frequently one of the hardest ever, and even if you are prepared, the pressure can feel so intense that you may find yourself wondering whether you made the right decision to pursue this career. A new institution, new colleagues, new students, the need to prove yourself, pressure to publish (and perhaps pressure to finish the dissertation), the paper you promised for AATSEEL, and possible family pressures if you have a spouse and family adjusting to a new situation too—and all while you are teaching two or three new courses each semester, frantically rereading your source material to stay a step ahead of the students, preparing lectures, grading papers—it may seem at times overwhelming.

1. Before you even start the job, finish your dissertation and do as much course preparation as possible!

You are likely to become overtired, frustrated at being unable to meet the standards you've imagined in the courses you are teaching, and at times profoundly discouraged.[2]

In fact, research has shown that academic success or failure can usually be traced to a few "turning points" or crucial events (real or perceived) that occur during the first year and cluster into four broad categories: collegial isolation, collegial disapproval, self-doubts about competence, and feelings of victimization and suspicion. If these kinds of experiences are anticipated, they can more easily be avoided.[3]

The Challenges

As difficult as it is to really understand the challenges before you experience them, it nonetheless helps to be aware of the common sources of stress for new faculty.

- First and foremost is *not enough time* to respond to the multiple pressures and demands on you: time for teaching and students; for research, writing, and publishing; for professional networking, conferences, and other demands; for

2. Patricia Chaput, *An Introduction to the Job Search: For Graduate Students in the Slavic Department* (Cambridge: Harvard University Slavic Department, 1993), 25.

3. See R. Boice, "Early Turning Points in Professional Careers of Women and Minorities," in *Building A Diverse Faculty*, ed. by J. Gainen and R. Boice (San Francisco: Jossey Bass, No. 53, Spring 1993): 71-79, and JoAnn Moody, "Junior Faculty: Job Stresses and How to Cope With Them," draft paper, New England Board of Higher Education's Doctoral and Dissertation Scholars Program, 1996. In addition to the aforementioned sources, see Robert Boice, *The New Faculty Member: Supporting and Fostering Professional Development* (San Francisco: Jossey-Bass Publishers, 1992), as summarized in JoAnn Moody, "Visualizing Yourself as a Successful Teacher, Writer, and Colleague," draft paper, New England Board of Higher Education's Doctoral and Dissertation Scholars Program, 1996. I am greatly indebted to Dr. Moody's and Professor Boice's work in informing the following discussion. See also Heiberger and Vick's *The Academic Job Search Handbook*.

administrative and other "citizenship" duties—not to mention for your outside life and relationships.

- *Unrealistic expectations*—yours for yourself or for the institution, or the institution's toward you—can also create great stress and frustration, since, by definition, you—or they—cannot deliver. For example, new faculty members usually overestimate the amount of time they will have available for their own research and writing, and underestimate the time required by teaching. Sometimes even realistic expectations may not be met, causing frustration and bitterness, for example, if certain resources promised by the department are not delivered.

- *Inadequate feedback and recognition* from colleagues are the norm in institutions of higher education, except at prescribed intervals (contract renewal, tenure decisions), and can cause anxiety for many new faculty members. This is related to *lack of collegiality*, another stressor characterizing many departments, which is caused by the culture of the department and/or the pressure of excessive demands on the faculty. Drawing appropriate boundaries between yourself and the students (especially graduate students, who may be older than you) can be challenging as well, particularly if you don't feel welcomed by your colleagues.

- Women and minorities may face *special obstacles and frustrations*: loneliness, a feeling of second-class citizenship, added pressure to prove themselves, excessive student demands, or extra demands for committee work as the token "whatever."

- Replacement or part-time faculty have the *added stress of being peripheral and temporary*, which is only partially offset by often being spared committee assignments. Here the challenge is to make yourself so indispensable and desirable as a colleague that the department will look for ways to create a tenure-track position.

Four Meta-Rules for Surviving the First Year

1. *Get your priorities straight and then stick to them!* You will need to clarify your professional priorities by considering the culture of the institution and the profession, and your own values. Equally important are your personal priorities—make a commitment to honor your "outside" life from the beginning and to strive for a balance with your professional life. We all know that "an academic's work is never done," so it is incumbent on *you* to stay focused, set some limits and boundaries, and learn to say NO! (Women should especially take heed, since they generally have a harder time saying no.)

As one successful academic reflected after she received tenure:

> [Y]ou are likely to be offered many opportunities. Don't feel compelled to take advantage of all of them. Be selective. *You* decide. Whatever you do, never believe for a moment that you are the only person who can do anything—no matter who tells you so. If you don't direct your own path, you will find yourself on someone else's journey.[4]

2. *Find mentors inside and outside your department and institution.* Go to them for concrete, specific advice on everything from how to handle a student to how best to allocate your time among teaching, research/writing, academic service, and professional network building. Unless you are lucky enough to have a mentor before you go (research shows that this is a powerful predictor of academic success for new faculty), you will undoubtedly have to take the initiative to establish these mentor relationships. *Also take the initiative to establish relationships with other colleagues both inside and outside your department.* Talk with them and solicit feedback on your ideas, proposals, papers, and teaching, and look for collaborative projects.

3. *Make a five-year plan* (checking it over with your mentors and department head) and learn and implement the principles of time

4. Dr. Arethra B. Pigford, "Scaling the Ivory Tower to Tenure and Promotion," *Black Issues in Higher Education* 12, no. 8 (June 15, 1995): 64.

management for your weekly, monthly, and semester goal-setting and planning. Revise the plan as you go along. Allocate at least two and preferably four to five hours a week during the semester to your writing. Also keep careful records of your activities and accomplishments, such as class grade lists, course outlines, notes and evaluations; copies of anything written for institutional business, publication, or public presentation; letters of commendation and reviews of your work; and grants. Keep your chair informed of these accomplishments.[5]

4. *Maintain a positive attitude.* Try to squelch your own negative self-talk, as well as the ceaseless complaints of colleagues. Try to give back to the community as well as to promote your own career. Strive "religiously" to incorporate a support network and stress reduction and other meaningful activities into your life.

Hang in there! Give it a chance. The years should get progressively less difficult and your professional and personal life much more manageable and satisfying.

5. This advice is taken from Melanie S. Gustafson, ed., *Becoming a Historian: A Survival Manual for Women and Men* (Washington, D.C.: American Historical Association, 1991), 64, and quoted in Moody, "Junior Faculty: Job Stresses and How to Cope With Them," 2-3.

Professional Associations

Academy of Management

P.O. Box 3020
Briarcliff Manor, NY 10510-8020
(914) 923-2607
(914) 923-2615 (fax)
aom@academy.pace.edu
http://aom.pace.edu/indextext.html
Convention held in August

American Academy of Religion

1703 Clifton Road, N.E.
Suite G-5
Atlanta, GA 30329-4075
(404) 727-7920
(404) 727-7959 (fax)
aar@emory.edu
http://scholar.cc.emory.edu/scripts/AAR/AAR-MENU.html
Convention held in November

American Anthropological Association

4350 North Fairfax Drive
Suite 640
Arlington, VA 22203-1620
(703) 528-1902
(703) 528-3546 (fax)
tcallin@ameranthassn.org
http://www.ameranthassn.org/
Convention held in November

American Association for the Advancement of Science
1200 New York Avenue, N.W.
Washington, DC 20005
(202) 326-6400
(202) 289-4021 (fax)
http://www.aaas.org/

American Association of Community Colleges
National Center for Higher Education
1 Dupont Circle, N.W.
Suite 410
Washington, DC 20036-1176
(202) 728-0200
(202) 833-2467 (fax)
mlatif@aacc.nche.edu
http://www.aacc.nche.edu/
Convention held in spring

American Association of State Colleges and Universities
1 Dupont Circle, N.W.
Suite 700
Washington, DC 20036-1192
(202) 293-7070
(202) 296-5819 (fax)
Conference held in November

American Association of University Professors
1012 14th Street, N.W.
Suite 500
Washington, DC 20005-3465
(202) 737-5900
(800) 424-2973
(202) 737-5526 (fax)
aaup@aaup.org
http://www.igc.apc.org/aaup/index.htm

American Association of University Women
1111 16th Street, N.W.
Washington, DC 20036
(202) 785-7700
(202) 872-1425 (fax)
info@mail.aauw.org
http://www.aauw.org/

American Astronomical Society
2000 Florida Avenue, N.W.
Suite 400
Washington, DC 20009
(202) 328-2010
(202) 234-2560 (fax)
aas@aas.org
http://www.aas.org/
Convention held in January and June

American Chemical Society
1155 16th Street, N.W.
Washington, DC 20036
(202) 872-4600
(202) 872-4615 (fax)
career@acs.org
gopher://acsinfo.acs.org/
http://www.acs.org/
Convention held in August

American Economic Association
2014 Broadway
Suite 305
Nashville, TN 37203
(615) 322-2595
(615) 343-7590 (fax)
aeainfo@ctrvax.vanderbilt.edu
http://www.vanderbilt.edu/AEA/
Convention held in December or January

American Educational Research Association
1230 17th Street, N.W.
Washington, DC 20036-3078
(202) 223-9485
(202) 775-1824 (fax)
aera@aera.net
http://aera.net/indextxt.html
Convention held in spring

American Folklore Society
c/o American Anthropological Association
4350 North Fairfax Drive
Suite 640
Arlington, VA 22203
(703) 528-1902
(703) 528-3546 (fax)
http://gopher.panam.edu:70/1gopher_root10%3a%5b000000%5d
Convention held in October

American Historical Association
400 A Street, S.E.
Washington, DC 20003-3889
(202) 544-2422
(202) 544-8307 (fax)
aha@theaha.org
http://chnm.gmu.edu/chnm/aha/
Convention held in January

American Institute of Biological Sciences
730 11th Street, N.W.
Washington, DC 20001-4521
(202) 628-1500
(202) 628-1509 (fax)
washington@AIBS.org
http://www.pslgroup.com/dg/3c36.htm
Convention held in August

American Institute of Chemical Engineers
345 E. 47th Street
New York, NY 10017-2395
(212) 705-7338
(212) 752-3294 (fax)
http://www.aiche.org/
Convention held three times a year

American Institute of Physics
1 Physics Ellipse
College Park, MD 20740-3843
(301) 209-3100
(301) 209-0843 (fax)
http://www.aip.org/

American Mathematical Society
Box 6248
Providence, RI 02940-6248
(401) 455-4000
(401) 331-3842 (fax)
ams@ams.org
gopher://e-math.ams.org
http://www.ams.org/
Convention held in January

American Musicological Society
201 S. 34th Street
Philadelphia, PA 19104-6313
(215) 898-8698
(215) 898-2106 (fax)
ams@mail.sas.upenn.edu
http://musdra.ucdavis.edu/documents/ams/ams.html
Convention held in October or November

American Philological Association
Department of Classics
Holy Cross College
Worcester, MA 01610
(508) 793-2203
(508) 793-3428 (fax)
Convention held in late December

American Philosophical Association
University of Delaware
Newark, DE 19716
(302) 831-1112
(302) 831-8690 (fax)
http://www.udel.edu/apa/
Three conventions a year: eastern U.S. in December,
West Coast in March, central U.S. in April

American Physical Society
1 Physics Ellipse
College Park, MD 20740-3844
(301) 209-3200
(301) 209-0865 (fax)
http://aps.org/
Convention held in March and April

American Planning Association
122 S. Michigan Avenue
Suite 1600
Chicago, IL 60603-9604
(312) 431-9100
(312) 431-9985 (fax)
http://planning.org/abtapa/abtapa.html
Convention held in March or April

American Political Science Association
1527 New Hampshire Avenue, N.W.
Washington, DC 20036
(202) 483-2512
(202) 483-2657 (fax)
apsa@apsanet.org
http://www.apsanet.org/
Convention held in August

American Psychological Association
750 First Street, N.E.
Washington, DC 20002-4242
(202) 336-5500
(202) 336-6069 (fax)
executiveoffice@apa.org
http://www.apa.org/
Convention held in August

American Society of Civil Engineers
1015 15th Street, N.W.
Suite 600
Washington, DC 20005
(202) 789-2200
(800) 548-2723
(202) 289-6797 (fax)
http://www.asce.org/
Convention held in October

American Sociological Association
1722 N Street, N.W.
Washington, DC 20036-2981
(202) 833-3410
(202) 785-0146 (fax)
executive.office@asanet.org
http://www.asanet.org/
Convention held in August

American Statistical Association
1429 Duke Street
Alexandria, VA 22314-3402
(703) 684-1221
(703) 684-2037 (fax)
asainfo@amstat.org
http://www.amstat.org/
Convention held in August

American Studies Association
1120 19th Street, N.W.
Suite 301
Washington, DC 20036
(202) 467-4783
(202) 467-4786 (fax)
pp001366@mindspring.com
http://www.georgetown.edu/crossroads/asainfo.html
Convention held in November

Archaeological Institute of America
656 Beacon Street
Boston, MA 02215-2010
(617) 353-9361
(617) 353-6550 (fax)
aia@bu.edu
http://csaws.brynmawr.edu:443/web2/index.html
Convention held in December

Associated Writing Programs
Tallwood House, Mail Stop 1E3
George Mason University
Fairfax, VA 22030
(703) 993-4301
(703) 993-4302 (fax)
http://web.gmu.edu/departments/awp/

Association for Asian Studies
1 Lane Hall
University of Michigan
Ann Arbor, MI 48109-1290
(313) 665-2490
(313) 665-3801 (fax)
postmaster@aasianst.org
http://www.easc.indiana.edu/~aas/
Convention held in spring

Association for Public Policy Analysis and Management
P.O. Box 18766
Washington, DC 20036
(202) 857-8788
(202) 466-3982 (fax)

Association for Theatre in Higher Education
200 N. Michigan Avenue
Suite 300
Chicago, IL 60601
(312) 541-2066
(312) 541-1271 (fax)
71005.1134@compuserve.com
Convention held in August

Association for Women in Science
1200 New York Avenue, N.W.
Suite 650
Washington, DC 20005
(202) 326-8940
(202) 408-8960 (fax)
awis@awis.org
http://www.awis.org/

Association of Collegiate Schools of Architecture
1735 New York Avenue, N.W.
3rd Floor
Washington, DC 20006
(202) 785-2324
(202) 628-0448 (fax)
sinclai@cc.umanitoba.ca
http://cad9.cadlab.umanitoba.ca/acsa/info.html
Convention held in March

College Art Association
275 Seventh Avenue
New York, NY 10001
(212) 691-1051
(212) 627-2381 (fax)
nyoffice@collegeart.org
http://sap.mit.edu/caa/
Convention time varies

Federation of American Societies for Experimental Biology
9650 Rockville Pike
Bethesda, MD 20814-3998
(301) 530-7000
(301) 571-0699 (fax)
fasebinfo@faseb.org
http://www.faseb.org/

Geological Society of America
3300 Penrose Place, Box 9140
Boulder, CO 80301
(303) 447-2020
(303) 447-1133 (fax)
admin@geosociety.org
http://aescon.com/geosociety/index.html
Convention held in October

Gerontological Society of America
1275 K Street, N.W.
Suite 350
Washington, DC 20005-4006
(202) 842-1275
(202) 842-1150 (fax)
geron@geron.org
http://www.geron.org/
Convention held in November

History of Science Society
Box 351330
University of Washington
Seattle, WA 98195-1330
(206) 543-9366
(206) 685-9544 (fax)
hssexec@u.washington.edu
http://weber.u.washington.edu/~hssexec/
Convention held in fall or December

Institute of Electrical and Electronics Engineers
345 E. 47th Street
New York, NY 10017
(212) 705-7900
(212) 705-7900 (fax)
http://www.ieee.org/

Linguistics Society of America
1325 18th Street, N.W.
Suite 211
Washington, DC 20036
(202) 835-1714
zzlsa@gallua.gallaudet.edu
Convention held in January

Materials Research Society
9800 McKnight Road
Pittsburgh, PA 15237-6006
(412) 367-3003
(412) 367-4373 (fax)
info@mrs.org
http://www.mrs.org/
Two conventions: West Coast convention held in spring,
East Coast convention held after Thanksgiving

Modern Language Association of America
10 Astor Place
New York, NY 10003
(212) 475-9500
(212) 477-9863 (fax)
info@mla.org
http://www.acls.org/mla.htm
Convention held in December

National Association for Ethnic Studies
Arizona State University
Department of English
P.O. Box 870302
Tempe, AZ 85287-0302
(602) 965-2197
(602) 965-3451 (fax)
NAESI@asuvm.inre.asu.edu
http://www.ksu.edu/ameth/naes/naes.htm

National Association for Humanities Education
University of Southwestern Louisiana
P.O. Box 44691
Lafayette, LA 70504-4961
(318) 482-6906
(318) 482-6195 (fax)

National Association for Women in Education
1325 18th Street, N.W.
Suite 210
Washington, DC 20036-6511
(202) 659-9330
(202) 457-0946 (fax)
nawe@clark.net
Conference held in March

Population Association of America
1722 N. Street, N.W.
Washington, DC 20036
(202) 429-0891
(202) 785-0146 (fax)
Convention held in spring

Regional Science Association International
1 Observatory
901 S. Mathews
University of Illinois
Urbana, IL 61801-3682
(217) 333-8904
(217) 333-3065 (fax)
RSAI@UIUC.EDU
http://www.staff.uiuc.edu/~bcarbonn/index.htm

Society for Industrial and Applied Mathematics
3600 University City Science Center
Philadelphia, PA 19104-2688
(215) 382-9800
(215) 386-7999 (fax)
siam@siam.org
http://www.siam.org/
Conference held in July

The Real World
(Professional Psychology Seminar)

The seminar will meet on Friday at 2:00 in the 7th floor conference room.

14 February. How to write a Ph.D. dissertation. Faculty will describe their experiences in writing the thesis and selecting their thesis committees, and will offer advice on fishing, cutting bait, and other useful skills.

21 February. Selling yourself. Where? University, research, industry, government. Postdocs versus real jobs. Networking at conferences. Also how to prepare a curriculum vitae. Students will be asked to prepare a vita in advance, which will then be analyzed by the group. Faculty will contribute copies of their vitae to be used as models. Dan Gilbert will visit.

28 February. How to deliver a job talk and survive a job interview. A mock job interview will be delivered and discussed. Visits by those recently at the job front.

7 March. How to negotiate a position. After a brief discussion, volunteers will participate in mock negotiations with the Chairman. These interactions will be analyzed by the group. Visit by our Chair Dan Schacter.

The Psychology Department of Harvard University has offered this for-credit seminar every two years since 1990.

14 March. How to publish articles and books. Difference between articles and chapters. What journals. Order of authorship. The importance of persistence and having a thick skin will be emphasized. Students will review copies of letters to faculty from editors of journals, and copies of responses to those letters. Jerry Kagan will consult.

21 March. How to write and revise a grant proposal. The best way to organize a proposal and tricks of the trade will be reviewed. Successful and unsuccessful proposals from faculty will be reviewed and analyzed.

4 April. How to review a journal article. Students will be asked to read a short preprint in advance, and to prepare a review. The reviews will then be reviewed and discussed.

11 April. [How to survive as a new faculty member.] Strategies for time sharing. Professors have three jobs: teaching (undergraduate and graduate), research, and administration. Vicissitudes of being the most recently arrived faculty member. Outlook for women and minority faculty. We will discuss survival techniques in this session that will allow you to perform each job without losing focus on what is important. Tips on running a lab. Nalani Ambadi will discuss the trials of succeeding while parenting as a junior faculty.

18 April. How to participate and be a good Departmental Citizen. Examples of appropriate and inappropriate strategies. Examples of good and bad behavior: ethics, fraud, and sexual harassment.

25 April. How to structure a course and plan the semester. Different ways of designing courses will be discussed.

Appendix Three

Some Tips for Approaching the Job Search in Dual-Career Families

1. Start early with self-assessment, and continue to pay attention to it, particularly regarding your values. You will need to set priorities, both as individuals and as a couple, among your work-related and other central values, especially family.

2. Start your career planning and job-search process early and jointly. Strive to think flexibly, broadly, and creatively. To be more specific, how flexible can each of you be in your type of work, depending on your field and interests (e.g., economics versus most humanities, or a specialty field versus broad discipline expertise)? Will you both go on the market at the same time? If not, how will you take into account the interests of the partner who job hunts later?

3. Start by each of you listing all the places where you could look for or might get a job, ranging from "good enough" to "wonderful." It is important to generate "good enough" possibilities. Use the concept of regions, not cities. Then look for the points of overlap in your lists.

4. Chances are that one partner has a strong geographical preference (e.g., an existing job), which the other will try his or her best to honor. But it's important for the spouse who already has a job to start investigating alternatives in the areas of the other's preference

This section has benefited from discussion in 1992 with Dr. Patricia Light, then Director of the Harvard Business School Counseling Office, and from the discussion in Heiberger and Vick, *The Academic Job Search Handbook*, 148-50.

early in the process, so that you as a couple are not faced at the end with an irreconcilable choice.

5. If one partner can't move (is this a joint decision?), think in terms of the regional area, alternative kinds of work, and a different career trajectory. Also explore the idea of a commuter marriage. Under what conditions would it be possible, if any? For how long? If you are considering jobs in separate locations, ask yourself: Can you afford two residences, large travel and phone bills, and the other inherent expenses? Who will do most of the commuting? How difficult is it to travel between the places you are considering? How difficult will it be to shift back and forth from being alone to being together?

6. Be creative with both job applications and negotiations—e.g., think about split positions, part-time positions, and positions elsewhere in the university or nearby. When and if it seems appropriate, enlist the aid of the search committee members, department chair, and/or dean in generating options for your spouse, asking particularly for academic jobs but also for nonacademic ones. Also consider asking for arrangements that would ameliorate the effects of commuting, such as consolidating teaching into three days a week, or one semester, or two of three quarters. (The timing of such requests is discussed in Chapter Five.)

7. When it comes to making a decision, face the issues openly, honestly, and thoroughly. How would you feel about turning this job down? Would you be likely to blame your spouse, or to harbor bitterness and resentment? How would you minimize regret? How would it be to have a transitional period in which you live apart? Have you exhausted all the alternatives? Listen to your intuition as well as to reason in considering these issues.

8. Keep evaluating your options and decisions as both of you move along in your professional careers and conditions change—for example, as you have children, change professional directions, or become better known in your fields.

Additional Reading and On-Line Resources

Publications

General

Anthony, Rebecca, and Gerald Roe. *The Curriculum Vitae Handbook: Using Your CV to Present and Promote Your Academic Career.* Iowa City: Rudi Publishing, 1994.

Anthony, Rebecca, and Gerald Roe. *Finding a Job in Your Field: A Handbook for Ph.D.'s and M.A.'s.* Princeton: Peterson's Guides, 1984.

ARIS
    Academic Research Information System
    (Up-to-date information on federal and private sources of grants, fellowships, scholarships, contracts and awards to colleges and universities, research centers, and individuals.)
    Academic Research Information System, Inc.
    2940 16th Street
    Suite 314
    San Francisco, CA 94103
    (415) 558-8133
    (415) 558-8135 (fax)
    arisnet@dnai.com
    http://www.arisnet.com

Boice, Robert. *The New Faculty Member: Supporting and Fostering Professional Development*. San Francisco: Jossey-Bass Publishers, 1992.

Bowen, William C., and Julie Anne Sosa. *Prospects for Faculty in the Arts and Sciences: A Study of Factors Affecting Demand and Supply, 1987 to 2012*. Princeton: Princeton University Press, 1989.

Chronicle of Higher Education
1255 23rd Street, NW
Washington, D.C. 20037
(202) 466-1000
(202) 296-2691 (fax)
http://chronicle.merit.edu/

Deneef, A.L., C.D. Goodwin, and E.S. McCrate, eds. *The Academic's Handbook*. London: Duke University Press, 1988.

Fisher, Roger, and William Ury, with Bruce Patton, ed. *Getting to Yes: Negotiating Agreement Without Giving In*. 2d ed. New York: Penguin Books, 1991.

Gleckner, Robert F. "A Taxonomy of Colleges and Universities." In *The Academic's Handbook*, edited by A. L. Deneef, C.D. Goodwin, and E.S. McCrate. London: Duke University Press, 1988.

Grant Advisor
The Grant Advisor
P.O. Box 520
Linden, VA 22642
info@grantadvisor.com
http://grantadvisor.com/

Harrington, Kevin, ed. *The Higher Education Job Search: A Guide for Prospective Faculty Members*. Evanston, Ill.: American Association for Employment in Education, Inc. (AAEE), 1997.

Heiberger, Mary Morris, and Julia Miller Vick. *The Academic Job Search Handbook*. 2d ed. Philadelphia: University of Pennsylvania Press, 1996.

Lingua Franca: The Review of Academic Life
Lingua Franca Inc.
172 E. Boston Post Road
Mamaroneck, NY 10543
(914) 698-9427
(914) 698-9488 (fax)

Marshall, Darrel R., and Judy A. Strother. *The Right Fit: An Educator's Career Handbook and Employment Guide.* Scottsdale: Gorusch Scarisbrick, 1990.

McDaniels, Carl. *Developing a Professional Vita or Resume.* Garrett Park: Garrett Park Press, 1990.

Merki, Mark, and Don Merki, Ph.D. *Jumping Through the Hoops: A Survival Guide to Graduate School.* Durham: Great Activities Publishing Company, 1995.

Miller, Joan I. and Bruce J. Taylor. *The Thesis Writer's Handbook: A Complete One Source Guide to Writers of Research Papers.* West Linn: Alcove Publishing Co., 1987.

Moody, JoAnn. "Junior Faculty: Job Stresses and How to Cope With Them," draft paper for the New England Board of Higher Education's Doctoral and Dissertation Scholars Program, 1996.

Moody, JoAnn. "Visualizing Yourself as a Successful Teacher, Writer, and Colleague," draft paper for the New England Board of Higher Education's Doctoral and Dissertation Scholars Program, 1996.

Moore, Richard W. *Winning the Ph.D. Game.* New York: Dodd, Mead & Co., 1985.

Newhouse, Margaret. *Outside The Ivory Tower: A Guide for Academics Considering Alternative Careers.* Cambridge: Office of Career Services, Faculty of Arts and Sciences, Harvard University, 1993.

Newhouse, Margaret. *Report on Ph.D. Recipients, 1995-96.* Cambridge: Office of Career Services, Faculty of Arts and Sciences, Harvard University, 1996.

Peters, R.L. *Getting What You Came For: The Smart Student's Guide to Earning a Master's or Ph.D.* New York: Noonday Press, 1992.

Rose, Suzanna, ed. *The Career Guide for Women Scholars.* Springer Series: Focus on Women, vol. 8. New York: Springer Pub. Co., 1986.

Rosovsky, Henry. *The University: An Owner's Manual.* New York: W.W. Norton, 1990.

Rudestam, Kjell E. and Rae R. Newton. *Surviving Your Dissertation: A Comprehensive Guide to Content and Process.* London and Newbury Park: SAGE Publications, 1992.

Schuster, Jack H. "Whither the Faculty? The Changing Academic Labor Market." *Educational Record* 76, no. 4 (fall 1995): 28-33.

Sternberg, David. *How to Complete and Survive a Doctoral Dissertation.* New York: St. Martin's Press, 1981.

Verba, Cynthia. *The Graduate Guide to Grants, The Harvard Guide to Dissertation Fellowships,* and *The Harvard Guide to Postdoctoral Fellowships.* Annual publications of the Harvard University Graduate School of Arts and Sciences, Cambridge, Mass.

Verba, Cynthia. *Scholarly Pursuits: A Practical Guide to Academe.* Rev. ed. Cambridge: Graduate School of Arts and Sciences, Harvard University, 1997.

Humanities

Chaput, Patricia. *An Introduction to the Job Search: For Graduate Students in the Slavic Department.* Cambridge: Harvard University Slavic Department, 1993.

Gustafson, Melanie S., ed. *Becoming a Historian: A Survival Manual for Women and Men.* Washington, D.C.: American Historical Association, 1991.

Schuster, Jack H. "Speculating about the Labor Market for Academic Humanists: 'Once More unto the Breach.'" In *Profession 95*. New York: The Modern Language Association of America, 1995.

Showalter, English. *A Career Guide for PhDs and PhD Candidates in English and Foreign Languages*. New York: Modern Language Association of America, 1985.

"Special Topic on the Job Market." In *Profession 94*. New York: Modern Language Association, 1994.

Sciences

Feibelman, Peter. *A Ph.D. Is Not Enough!* Reading: Addison-Wesley Publishing Company, 1993.

Fiske, Peter S. *To Boldly Go: A Practical Career Guide for Scientists*. Washington, D.C.: American Geophysical Union, 1996.

Massy, William F. and Charles A. Goldman. *The Production and Utilization of Science and Engineering Doctorates in the U.S.* Palo Alto: Stanford Institute for Higher Education Research, 1995.

Reis, Richard M. *Tomorrow's Professor: Preparing for Academic Careers in Sciences and Engineering*. Piscataway, N.J.: IEEE Press, 1997.

Smith, Robert V. *Graduate Research: A Guide for Students in the Sciences*. 2d ed. New York: Plenum Publishing Corporation, 1990.

Social Sciences

Brams, Christianne, Claudia Lampman, and Mark E. Johnson. "Preparation of Applications for Academic Positions in Psychology." *American Psychologist* 50, no. 7 (July 1995): 533-538.

Carson, Richard and Peter Navarro, "A Seller's and Buyer's Guide to the Job Market for Beginning Academic Economists." *Journal of Economic Perspectives* 2, no. 2 (Spring 1988): 132-148.

Women's and Minority Issues

Black Issues in Higher Education
Cox Matthews & Associates, Inc.
10520 Warwick Avenue
Suite B-8
Fairfax, VA 22030
tel: (703) 385-2981
fax: (703) 385-1839

Boice, R. "Early Turning Points in Professional Careers of Women and Minorities." In *Building a Diverse Faculty*, edited by J. Gainen and R. Boice. San Francisco: Jossey Bass, No. 53, Spring 1993.

Caplan, Paula J. *Lifting a Ton of Feathers: A Woman's Guide to Surviving in an Academic World*. Toronto: University of Toronto Press, 1994.

Pigford, Dr. Arethra B. "Scaling the Ivory Tower to Tenure and Promotion." *Black Issues in Higher Education* 12, no. 8 (June 15, 1995): 64.

On-Line Resources[1]

Job Listings

The Chronicle of Higher Education
http://chronicle.merit.edu/

Jobs in Higher Education
http://volvo.gslis.utexas.edu/~acadres/jobs/index.html

Academic Position Network
http://www.umn.edu/apn/
gopher://wcni.cis.umn.edu:11111/

---

1. Several of the on-line listings here come from Kevin Harrington, ed., *The Higher Education Job Search*. Please note that on-line resources change frequently.

Education Jobs Page
http://www.nationjob.com/education

Academic Employment Network
http://www.academploy.com/

FedWorld Federal Job Search
http://www.fedworld.gov/jobs/jobsearch.html

General Information

The Center for All Collegiate Information
http://www.collegiate.net/

National Teaching and Learning Forum
http://www.ntlf.com/

Peterson's Education & Career Center
http://www.petersons.com/

The Riley Guide
http://www.dbm.com/jobguide/

Academic Salary Information

National Teaching and Learning Forum
College and University Interactive Faculty Database
http://tikkun.ed.asu.edu/aaup/

Faculty Salaries of Public Institutions in the AAU
http://osshe.edu/irs/factbook/faculty/aaupub.htm

University of California Academic Salary Scales
http://www.ucop.edu/acadadv/acadpers/faccont.html

California State University System Salary Structure
http://csueb.sfsu.edu/csueb/salary.html

Notes

Notes

Notes

Notes

Notes

Notes

Notes

Notes